THE GRASS
ROOTS PEOPLE

AN AMERICAN REQUIEM

THE GRASS ROOTS PEOPLE

Written and Photographed by Nancy Wood

Harper & Row, Publishers
New York,
Hagerstown,
San Francisco,
London

THE GRASS ROOTS PEOPLE. Copyright © 1978 by Nancy Wood.
All rights reserved. Printed in the United States of America. No
part of this book may be used or reproduced in any manner
whatsoever without written permission except in the case of brief
quotations embodied in critical articles and reviews. For infor-
mation address Harper & Row, Publishers, Inc., 10 East 53rd
Street, New York, N.Y. 10022. Published simultaneously in Can-
ada by Fitzhenry & Whiteside Limited, Toronto.

FIRST EDITION

Designed by Stephanie Tevonian

Library of Congress Cataloging in Publication Data

Wood, Nancy C
  The grass roots people.

  1. Rocky Mountain region—Social life and customs.
I. Title.
F721.W66 1978   978   76-26258
ISBN 0-06-014734-2

78   79   80   81   82   10   9   8   7   6   5   4   3   2   1

For Roy Stryker
who taught me the art of seeing

CONTENTS

INTRODUCTION

Late in 1970, I stood along the banks of the Purgatoire River in Colorado and watched a small town dying. Up and down the potholed streets of Sopris, where four generations of Italian coal miners and their families had lived and died, the people were moving out. The pickup trucks and the U-Hauls were loaded with artifacts of unnoticed lives; the automobiles had women in them who had cried too much already and children who kept looking back as the automobiles drove out of town for the last time.

Along the streets, the vacant houses were left unlocked; the bread ovens in the backyards were gape-mouthed and cold; here and there was washing forgotten on the line. East of town, the Army Corps of Engineers had already erected the dam intake tower and it loomed two hundred feet in the air, the castle insignia impudently crowning the top. As the people moved out, the bulldozers went to work, scraping up the streets and sidewalks and backyards of Sopris to make a giant earth-filled dam. The houses were of no use to them, so they were knocked down; the big yellow bulldozers rammed them again and again until at last they fell, the dust from the old walls escaping along with whatever memories were left.

I had no camera in 1970 and what I saw was recorded only in my mind. I remember the faces especially—mine-ruined old men who had made wine all their lives in the cellars of the houses; stoic old women who had lived through strikes and mine disasters; and a whole generation of children who would grow up somewhere else. I remember the details of those lives too—a rag doll dropped in the dust, a wine barrel left to rot, an apron draped across a discarded kitchen chair, a calendar turned back to 1965—the year that news of the dam first came.

Something important died at Sopris. Rural life, as I had observed it there and elsewhere in the state, was disappearing fast; busting the soil and breaking one's back were no longer relevant, whether it was in Colorado or two thousand miles away in Vermont. What special qualities did this life have? What were its strengths—and drawbacks? What was happening on the land, and in the small towns that dotted it? Many of the answers came from a special man, then in his declining years.

In 1962 I had begun a friendship with Roy Stryker, the gifted, farsighted director of the Farm Security Administration photography project of the thirties. Under his guidance, a priceless collection of 270,000 pictures of rural American life were taken by some of the greatest photographers of our time—Walker Evans, Dorothea Lange, Ben Shahn, Arthur Rothstein, Jack Delano, Russell Lee, John Vachon, Marion Post Wolcott and Carl Mydans. Stryker moved back to Colorado that year, and he and I spent countless hours looking through his personal file of FSA pictures. We talked about everything—photography, history and the American West, which we both loved so much.

Eventually he and I joined our efforts in a book, *In This Proud Land*, based on his own collection of FSA photographs, and I became his last pupil. He taught me how to see, and because of this, I decided to photograph the disappearing West in which I lived.

I read and reread Stryker's famous "shooting scripts," sent out to his photographers in the field as guidelines toward building the "human aspect" of a government file. He would tell them to shoot backyards, pool halls, bus stations, barbershops, bars, signs, highways, street corners, stores, schools, blacksmiths, old couples, families and what he called "the significant detail." To my astonishment, much of the material was as valid in the seventies as it had been in the thirties.

In February 1976, the Colorado Centennial-Bicentennial Commission awarded me a twelve-thousand-dollar grant to document rural life in Colorado for the Centennial; I would also take notes and present a permanent exhibition to the State Historical Society. In the next year and a half, I traveled more than fifteen thousand miles, shot over twelve thousand photographs, and came to know people as tough and varied as any who might have been encountered in the FSA days. These are the grass roots people, and they are the nation's backbone. There are not many of them left, and the kind of life they lead is, if not doomed, then precariously on the edge. In their prejudice, pride and patriotism they have also anchored rural life in a nineteenth-century framework which the rest of us call "quaint."

But there is more to them than that. In the gold mines and the bean fields, on cattle drives and wild horse hunts, at small-town fairs and rodeos, in one-room schoolhouses and neon-lighted cafés, at brandings, weddings and farm auctions, I have watched their underlying joy of life. It has nothing to do with money, which they are short of; they care about the constants: freshly turned wheat fields, cattle grazing on endless prairie lands, even the ageless stupidity of sheep, tended by the simplest of men. There is promise in young girls who raise 4-H Club calves; there is reassurance in young men who reap what their fathers have sown; there is comfort in the fact that farm women still prefer children, housework and church to other alternatives in life. These places, these lives, their past, their present, their uncertain future, are what I hope to have captured in this book.

I wish I had had a camera when Sopris died.

Nancy Wood
Ramah, Colorado
May 1978

PLAINS

The drought had no one dramatic day that stood out from all the rest. It went on in the same terrifying way all fall and winter, the sharp northwest winds rising and falling, settling the dust and stirring it again. The dust storms rose, two miles high and dirty brown, ripping the winter wheat crop from drought-bleached furrows, scouring the land and drying out whatever hope the people had left.

In Cheyenne Wells, the tumbleweeds piled up fifteen feet high on the courthouse lawn.

Not far from there, a farmer dug post holes four feet deep in the sandy soil and said there was no subsoil moisture.

Across the state line, a mail truck blew off the road and the postman had to radio for help.

In Yuma County, housewives strung rope between house and barn so the children would not get lost while doing chores.

In Cheyenne County, one bankrupt farmer drove his tractor to his fence line and walked away.

In Calhan, at St. Mary's Orthodox Church, a rain prayer was offered every Sunday: "O Lord Almighty, who has scattered the clouds over all the ends of the earth, we ask that you create a tempest with rain. Send forth the wind from your heavenly treasury, gather the waters from the seas and let them pour down upon the face of this earth . . . for it is only with moisture that we are able to grow food for ourselves and for our animals. . . ."

The farmers said:

"I've seen it worse and I'll live to see it worse again. When it's a bad year, you have trouble remembering the good. When it's good, you forget about the bad. When it's all you've got, you make the most of things."

"They are a proud people in this country. My father told me about a man during the Depression who climbed into his haystack and starved to death rather than ask his neighbors for help."

Sparse faces mirror a sparse land. What dries up on the outside shrivels the interior as well. When the land is wet, the memory freshens.

"If a man's got land, he don't need nothin' else."

"Dumb farmers is all we are. How come we don't unionize and go on strike?"

"I heard of a fellow once who just set out there in his wheat field screaming back at the wind. It didn't help much. Made him feel better, though."

"I lost everything three times. Three times came back. Now's the fourth. It's too late for me to come back again, but I'm going to do it anyhow."

The grass roots people wear their stubbornness like a badge, to set themselves apart from city people, whose confined and regimented lives they disdain. Out here, they seem to say, we have a freedom all our own. That the price of freedom involves backbreaking work, a constant battle with the elements and a steadily declining agricultural economy worries them not. In the little prairie towns with their porch swings, church picnics, unlocked doors and backyard politics; on the dried-up farms with half a century of worn-out machinery rusting in heaps around them; and on the mortgaged

ranches where the man on horseback remains the national symbol of independence, there is still a life that says "America" best. Call it pride or leaving one's mark; the grass roots people have coined the phrase "proved out."

In the deceptive calm between dust storms, the wheat farmers hurried outside and chiseled their soil to keep it from blowing away. Where drought has been it will come again, they said, bandannas around their faces to keep the dust out. But it was no use. The dust went into their lungs, the same as always, and the wind blew again as it had for six straight months, and the little piles of dirt they had mounded up soon blew away, out and over the land in thick, dark clouds.

Then the wind changed.

Curtis Schrimp sat in the window of his vintage Conoco station in Wild Horse, population twelve, and watched the red, angry dust move in from the south. "It's just what blew off into Kansas last month coming back," he observed.

His wife, Leona, wiped her glasses with a clean white apron and said, "It's uncomfortable and people are losing money, but I wouldn't say it's a disaster area. Not yet anyway. Why, there's wheat out there with roots as big as this." And she held up her fist to show how big the roots of the wheat plants really were.

Along U.S. 40, which runs eastward into Kansas and westward into Denver, the trucks drove with their lights on all day. Coming through Wild Horse, they honked their horns at Curtis Schrimp the way they always did. But they no longer stopped at Leona's Café for a piece of homemade pie or the thick hamburgers

Top left. *Mr. and Mrs. Walter Burns, Agate. "Been a rancher all my life, but emphysema's got me now."*

Bottom left. *Joe Maul, barber, Calhan. He has had his barbershop since 1956 in a remodeled harness shop.*

Above. *Boots Brinkley, roper at the Elbert County Fair.*

that people still talked about.

"I miss them," she said sadly, struggling through the dust storm to the locked door of the café she ran from 1937 to 1975. "But my legs gave out. I was up every day at five-thirty to open the café at six and I had the station to run when Curtis was driving the school bus. I went

Curtis Schrimp and his wife, Leona, Wild Horse. "I've had this station so long I could go out there and pump gas in my sleep."
Top right. *Wild Horse schoolhouse is now used by a local women's group.*

back and forth all day, between the house, the station and the café. I must have walked a thousand miles a year."

The café in which she had spent so much of her life was dark and filled with dust which had seeped through the cracks and the hole in the ceiling. Even though the café had been closed for two years, Leona still wiped the counter out of habit. "You wipe the same old counter for forty years and you can't stand to see it like this," she said, stirring the dust with a cloth. In the kitchen, Leona's dependable old iron stove stood with a patina of dust over it; the utensils were where she had left them, the handles worn smooth from her touch. The linoleum floor in front of the stove, where she had stood for so many years, her feet encased in sturdy leather shoes, was rubbed clean of its pattern.

"You could come in here and get a decent

19

meal for eighty cents. One pork chop. It was a dollar for two. I had a big family table over there and an old wood stove in the middle. It was nice." The harder she wiped the more she remembered. "A café is not just a place to eat. It's a place to get to know one another. I met more people passing through than most folks do in a lifetime."

Leona Schrimp, who had lived in Wild Horse all her life, stopped and thought about it. "It's a fact," she decided. And then: "People are still passing through. But no one ever stops. There's nothing to stop here for."

The blizzard struck suddenly in mid-March, on a Thursday afternoon, with winds of a hundred miles an hour. In the little prairie towns the people listened to the radio and wondered about it. Heavy snow warning. Stockmen's advisory. With calving already begun on most ranches, it could be a problem. But not too bad, they decided. Not the way it was during the winter of '72–73, when the chill factor was eighty below. That year, cattle died by the thousands and cattlemen went broke by the hundreds. You could expect a disaster like that maybe once in twenty years. Still, they were uneasy. Gathered around the gas stations and cafés, the hardware stores and the barbershops, the ranchers and the farmers on the eastern plains began to worry about what might happen when the first big flakes started coming down.

When the snow stopped two days later, nearly sixty thousand head of livestock lay dead in the hard-hit eastern counties. Four thousand miles of fence were down. Property damage ran

Opposite. *John Brittingham and Ted Evanoika carry two orphan calves through the snow. They will be bottle fed for several months, then sent to the livestock sale.*

Above. *Windmill repair occurs frequently, involves pulling twenty-one-foot-long joints of pipe out of the ground to get at sucker rods inside. This well is 168 feet deep, took one day to repair.*

over $42 million. Three schoolchildren froze to death in a field south of Ramah, trying to go from one girl's house to another's. Two men suffocated in their truck along U.S. 24. Everywhere, the snow drifted, twenty and thirty feet deep, up and over the houses and barns, knocking down fences, blocking every road in an area of more than ten thousand square miles. Cattle suffocated and froze and their bloated bodies were found against the fences when the snow melted. One rancher lost nine hundred head, which had gathered on a frozen lake and fallen through. The cattle that survived were found with their eyes frozen shut, ears frozen off, and hindquarters bare from the savage winds which had blasted off all their hair. Neighbors took in neighbors stranded miles from home; schoolchildren stayed with teachers and with bus drivers; motorists found themselves fed by strangers and bedded down in police stations and church halls. With electricity off for as long as nine days, ranch wives saved the contents of their freezers by canning everything on two-burner gas hot plates. In Eads, the locker plant, which had its own generator, let people store their food for nothing. And all across the land, ranchers began digging out half-dead cattle, stranded without food or water for as long as a week.

Yet when it was all over, the blizzard left little moisture except in the places where it had drifted. The rest of the land was as dry and dusty as ever. And the banks, which routinely handed out operating loans of $100,000 or more each spring, began to refuse even long-time applicants.

In Idalia, near the Colorado-Kansas line, Charles Andrews watched as the accumulations of a lifetime, spread out on the ground, were sold to fellow farmers at auction. That year, 22,000 American farmers lost their land at auction, and Andrews was one of them. The number of farms now stands at 2.8 million, half the number there were twenty-five years ago. In addition, every year a quarter of a million acres of cropland are gobbled up by urban development, highways and shopping centers.

"I never thought it would get this bad," Andrews said, watching a neighbor examine a set of tools he had had for twenty years.

Troil Welton, the auctioneer, moved among the crowd. "Here's a pile of gaskets. Who'll give me four bits?" A hand shot up and Welton shouted "Sold," then picked up some pipe and began to chant the familiar requiem.

Andrews turned away. "Maybe I can start over," he said, not really knowing how to go about it anymore.

"We never wanted to get rich," said his wife, noticing the leg that was coming off the kitchen chair that Welton was holding in the air. "We only wanted to make a living. We wanted to keep a-goin'."

"Here's a farmer who shouldn't have to quit," a neighbor said sympathetically, and told how Andrews was a better farmer than most. "Just hard luck was all."

Hard luck or not, the bank had refused to renew Andrews' note, forcing him to sell out. The trucks and the harvest equipment went at auction; so did all his cattle and 350 acres of land, the same land that his grandfather had homesteaded in the late 1800s. Eighty-four dollars an acre. Worth a hundred or more in a good

Farm auction, Ramah.

year. This was not a good year.

At day's end, Charles Andrews was only a few hundred dollars short of the $100,000 he needed to pay off his loan. At forty-seven, he wondered what he would do with his life, reduced now to one tractor and a few acres of land. "Been a farmer all my life till now," he said. "There's not a whole lot else I know how to do."

When the pickups were loaded with the artifacts of Charles Andrews' existence, Troil Welton waited until the farmer went inside. "I never saw a man take it so hard. He just sat there and watched it all go by." He shook his head sadly because Andrews, like most of his sellers, was an old friend.

For thirty-two years Troil Welton has seen people's lives coming and going on the auction block as old friends die or move to town, abandoning what is old, worn out or discarded.

Sometimes, when he cannot get a bid, the auctioneer buys the item himself. On his six-hundred-acre farm near Wray, Welton has built a huge metal garage to house it all. There are wringer washing machines and wood stoves; Farmall tractor wheels and rusted hand plows; milk pails and corn planters; an ancient truck chassis and a half-ton cannon; there are metal gates and cattle chutes; windmill blades, oxen yokes, barrel staves and leather harnesses. In Troil Welton's garage are hard facts and a soft heart, and it is neither good nor bad; it is just the way things turned out.

"In the Depression, you figured it took five failures to get a man off his farm," Welton said. "Now it takes one. If things don't get better, you'll see a lot more sales like this."

He watched Charles Andrews come toward him, seeming older and more stooped than he had at the beginning of the day. His shoulders

24

were set, not so much against the wind stirring out of the north as against the emptiness of the yard where his things had been.

"It's strange," the auctioneer said, making room for Charles Andrews to sit down. "Whenever you sell a sale, you sell something of the man along with it."

"There's no man that's had it harder than me. No man," said the seventy-two-year-old farmer, standing at the edge of his bean fields in the Arkansas valley. "I've got only two months to make a dollar—August and September. The other ten I pray. If the crop's been good, I get by a little. I went broke in '73 and again in '74. Three hailstorms ruined me. It took me twelve years to make some money and then I lost fifty thousand dollars to the hail.

"I don't know if we're gonna make it anymore. I only own ten acres and rent this other fifty. The only help I got are those three men that come up from Mexico every March and stay until October. Maybe it's illegal, but what else am I gonna do?

"Like I said, I was born in Italy. My father worked all his life in the zinc smelter. I went to farming in '21, backed with Mafia money. Oh, I didn't have to do anything for it. They wanted to make an investment and it was easier than goin' to the bank, but I never got mixed up in crime. No, I was just a poor dirt farmer, that's all.

"You see those three men over there pickin' corn? It's 180 degrees in those corn fields right now. The air just doesn't get in. But they're used to it. We've got tomatoes and beans and

Mexican bean picker earns about $4.60 per hour—if he is able to pick seventy-five pounds.

cantaloupes too, and it's not so hot pickin' them. They have to work from six in the morning till dark for nearly half the year, but what they make they send back to their families and it's more than they could make down there. I give 'em a place to live and it's better than most, with electricity and all.

"The faster they pick, the more they get paid. They get twenty-five cents a sack for corn and six cents a pound for beans, but they can

Pausing for a lunch of tortillas and beans, a worker says he would be a "poor peasant" in Mexico; he considers himself "worth a lot of money" here.

pick a hundred fifty pounds in two hours if they keep at it. They get paid for hoeing weeds, thinning tomatoes and corn, and cleaning ditches. I tell you, they're workers. I pay them by the acre—contract work it's called—and they get thirty dollars an acre to weed my onion field.

"They got machines now that can pick sweet corn, cucumbers, tomatoes and green beans. The corn picker costs fifty thousand, but it picks only corn. These three Mexicans, they'll pick anything, and a whole lot cheaper too."

Before the sodbusters came, there were Indians here, Cheyennes and Arapahos, and they moved about after the buffalo. Long before the Indians, there were dinosaurs, and before that, a shallow sea. Even now there is the imprint of the sea upon the land, but the water has dried up, leaving only shapes to suggest what might have been. The prairie is like the sea and the people roll and pitch with it; their eyes, like those of seafarers, are accustomed to looking long distances. Their eyes are forever on the sky, waiting for the rain that is always falling somewhere else.

There are facts to this land, but they do not tell the true story; they only mark events and places, offer dates as proof that history happened here and got recorded in all the books. The facts don't say that a man never wanted to quit when things got tough, not when he had every last dime staked on the land and refused to believe, even in the worst of times, that the weather had won and always would. Every twenty years, you could count on a drought that would last five to seven years. And drought was always followed by flood. If you could remember those two facts, could keep alive against it, could keep the women from going crazy, could see even half of the children live to grow up, could have the smallest victory now and then, then maybe you would turn out all right. In that land which negated all belief, you had to believe in what you could do if given half a chance.

The bones of Indians and buffalo and war

An Eastern Orthodox church and graveyard lie at a lonely crossroads on the plains of eastern Colorado.

ponies lie beneath the soil. Sometimes when the wind blows hard, a moan comes up over the prairie; the eerie sound rises and falls, pierces the night and shakes the windowpanes. The pragmatists say it is only the wind, but the old-timers listen with an ear for history. No, they say, it's an old chief crying.

And they look out their windows at the vast brown land as if to see a line of braves coming out of it.

There is a presence on this prairie. Not just of the Indians who perished at the end of the white man's gun, nor of the buffalo slaughtered for their hides. That sorrow rides the wind and crowds the dust, hides in the houses of the living and plays with the memory of the dead. This is a much more recent presence and it creeps out over the land from the deserted homesteads, the one-room schoolhouses and the wooden, belfried churches, whose bells

have all been stolen. There are ghosts among old boards creaking in the wind and a story to be told in windmills that stopped turning before the century had even begun. The prairie has its secrets. In rusted horse-drawn plows embedded in fields that just dried up. In fences painstakingly made of hand-cut posts laid out for five straight miles. In houses with porches put on for a view. In dormer windows out of which a young girl leaned, trying to see her suitor coming down the dusty road from the farm next door. Perhaps they married. Perhaps they did not. The old boards know. So much effort wasted and not a soul to know how many years passed before this family finally starved out. How many survived—and how many lie in the little cemetery at the top of the hill, where most of the markers have fallen down? The dust is already covering those futile proclamations of lifetimes spent in so much trying. For what? the

relentless wind seems to ask. For what?

Just to raise a good bunch of kids.

Just so we wouldn't starve.

We wanted to prove out.

The old stones stand in the graveyard adjoining the lonely white church set out on the open prairie fifteen miles from town.

"He was a farmer first and a husband second. That's why he was able to leave his wife and take a job near Stratton when he got blowed out. He came back eventually, but she was already gone. He got his beans in, though, and the alfalfa after that."

"There are children here who died before they lived. Diphtheria. Smallpox. Influenza. Cholera. Sometimes whole families went. The women who buried all their children went wild with grief. Like as not, we buried them before the year was out."

"The funeral was very small. There was just me and my brothers. Maybe an aunt or two. We

Top left. *Cemetery, Simla.*

Bottom left. *A newborn colt, steadied by John Brittingham, fascinates his stepdaughter, India Wood.*

Above. *Wedding of Joanne Burns and hog farmer Willard Boetger of Hugo. All the women's and girls' dresses were made by the bride and her sisters.*

gathered around the cemetery, waiting for the preacher to come. It was late and we all had to get back to the fields. The undertaker had just left us there, with the casket sitting on top of the ground. We couldn't go off and leave it and we couldn't stay either. Finally Henry, who was the oldest, got up and said, 'This here was Dad. He was born into this life and he died out of it. May God have mercy on his soul. Amen.' And that's all there was to it. The boys and me grabbed shovels and buried him ourselves. Afterwards, we all went home and had dinner."

They have sprung from the earth, this proud and anachronistic group of people who drive pickups with bumper stickers that say "God

Above. *Fred Lindley, a traveling salesman from Strasburg, drives more than 30,000 miles a year to sell his Rawleigh products to ranch wives.*
Top right. *Simla.*
Bottom right. *Nichols Tool Company, Simla.*

Bless John Wayne," "Steer Wrestlers Do It Better in the Dirt" and "Hungry and Out of Work? Eat an Environmentalist." They have a deep and natural sense of place, and that is what makes them different—and acceptable in spite of their tight-mindedness. In them is a genuine feeling of prerogative and continuity, of belonging here and nowhere else. Their roots go back into the land no more than a hundred years, yet they have developed a richness of character that sets them apart, a distinct physical appearance that marks them, as another bumper sticker says, "Proud to Be Country."

Hard and brittle as the land itself, with skin the color of the weathered prairie grass, with backs bent from a lifetime of walking into the wind, eyes reddened and teeth worn down from chewing on the grit that blows in, the plains people are a natural extension of the land. They look like the people on television and in the movies who play the parts of frontier characters, only they have come by their ways naturally. They represent the frontier dream we still long to believe in; but one can no longer buy a little farm or ranch and make a living at it. Back to the land requires cash in the bank; do-it-yourself is translated best through outside income or a job in town.

The Nichols Tool Company occupies over a block in the middle of "downtown" Simla, a small ranching community settled in the late 1880s, when the Rock Island Railroad was extended through the territory; it was given its name by the wife of a railroad official, who happened to be reading a book on India. Nichols Tool has been in Simla since 1933, when William Nichols came from Denver and opened a blacksmith shop in the depths of the Depression. Today Nichols uses five hundred tons of steel a year, and employs sixty men working two shifts in a huge corrugated building where giant machines roar, hiss and belch out of their fiery interiors replacement parts for farm machines. The workers make around four dollars

Twenty-three-year-old Turner Smith, foreground, works at Nichols Tool in order to afford a ranch.

an hour, considerably more than they could make pumping gas or working on a ranch. Some have been there as long as twenty years, but most are young men from the surrounding countryside who consider the job temporary.

"You got to have a dream, else what's the point of workin' a job like this?" said twenty-four-year-old Hank Dennard, who has a wife and two daughters. As the cooling plowshares came up out of a water bath, Dennard piled them on a conveyor belt.

"I bought 160 acres south of Yoder and paid for it with this job," he said, his smooth, round face reflecting what hope he had. "In another year I can buy another quarter section somewhere else. In two years I ought to be able to buy two more, someplace where it's still cheap, say fifty dollars an acre. Then, when I get a section together, maybe I can sell it and get something all in one place. No, I can't buy any more

land where I am. The big landowners have got it all." He shrugged to indicate that life had come to that now, with corporations and wealthy individuals seeking ranches as tax shelters.

"I do what a lot of people do," said twenty-three-year-old Turner Smith, stopping for a Coke at break time. "I bought my cattle first, then leased the land." Raised on a ranch near Ramah, Smith said he could not afford to buy any property of his own. "My dad has a pretty good place. When he retires I'll probably get some of his." Smith, unlike the rest, had only to bide his time.

Mike Pasko was twenty-four and he had been at Nichols for three years. "I bought my first Hereford herd three years ago," he said. "Fifteen registered heifers and one registered bull, plus twenty-one cows and calves." He ran them on four hundred acres that had belonged to his father, who had worked at Nichols for seventeen years before he died in 1973. But still, four hundred acres and thirty-seven head of cattle were not enough to live on. "My old man always thought he was going to be able to quit this job and make a living raising cattle. He never did. Well, I think I can do it, even if it takes me thirty years."

For forty-eight-year-old George Martin it was a different story. "I've got 960 acres that I'm leasing," he said. "For twenty years I've wanted to buy that land bad. I remember back in '60, when it was only twenty-five dollars an acre and I went to the land bank for a loan. I had a good job and everything and I showed them how I could make it pay, but they weren't interested. Right now the owner is asking $180 an acre for it. Oh, he'll get it, that's for sure. He'll be sitting pretty, and me, I guess I'll have to go on leasing other people's land."

The obsession to own land has been an American tradition throughout its white-supremecist history. The Homestead Act of 1862 was written to open the burgeoning West to settlement by offering 160 free acres to anyone who would "prove up" on it, a euphemism which often meant nothing more than erecting a tent or planting a few trees; it also meant filing homestead claims in the names of dead family members in order to amass as much free land as possible. Although President Andrew Johnson estimated that it would take six hundred years to settle the vast Western lands, it in fact took less than thirty.

But if the days of free land and cheap land are long gone, there are still those who will sac-

Terry Kelsey is a rancher with three careers—Longhorns, sculpture and aviation.

rifice nearly anything in order not only to own a chunk of ranch land but to enjoy the privacy that goes with it.

Around Elbert County, where he lives, thirty-one-year-old rancher Terry Kelsey is known as a man with three separate careers but only one true vocation—the immortalization of a Western life style that is largely of the past. When he was growing up on a ranch in Montana, Kelsey decided that the only thing he

Top right. *Sid Kelsey watches apprehensively as her husband, Terry, brands a Longhorn calf.*
Bottom right. *Terry Kelsey measures the horns of a favorite cow, Hurricane, while rancher David Bradley looks on.*

wanted to do with his life was to live it like a nineteenth-century cowboy, and so he has—feeding with a team in winter, bronc riding in rodeos in summer, shoeing and breaking horses, and raising prize-winning Texas longhorns. He and his wife, Sidni, whom he married when they were both eighteen and just out of high school, live in a log house they built themselves and have furnished with frontier furniture scrounged from auctions, basements and friends. Because he likes the idea of the West as it used to be, Kelsey has also collected and restored an Oliver buckboard, a horse-drawn sleigh and an ancient chuck wagon, which he keeps under cover next to his stack of winter hay. Grazing nearby are a pair of 1,800-pound shire horses, used to pull his feed wagon in winter.

To help pay off the 1,880-acre ranch he bought in 1973 for $240,000, Kelsey does Western sculpture. Breaking horses and saddle-bronc riding have left him with broken legs, arms, ribs and collarbone, and a split head, to say nothing of the time when the young shires ran away six times the first day they were in harness. But it is this firsthand knowledge that enables Kelsey to capture in bronze the complexities of a horse "snubbing" a colt, a cowboy using a Johnny Blocker loop or trying to front-foot a bronc on the ground. In sculpture, as in life, he knows how to drape the reins, tie the straps and fly the strings; he also sits by the

hour studying animals for muscle conformation.

Yet even with the brisk sale of his artwork, Kelsey cannot make enough to pay for his ranch or to raise the prestigious Longhorns, currently in demand as an exotic breed which command about four times more money than conventional cattle. Since 1967 Kelsey has worked for United Airlines, and two or three times a week he dons his pilot's uniform and drives sixty-five miles to Denver to board the 727 jet he flies as second officer. He detests working for the airline because it robs him of precious time he would rather spend with his bronzes or his cattle, but he cannot afford to give up his $22,000 annual salary just yet.

"In a year or two I'll be able to quit," he said one day, trimming the hoofs of his favorite horse, Sage. Already his land has nearly doubled in value, but the sale of his ranch is not foremost on his mind." I want to make it with art and I want to make it with Longhorns. I don't want to make it in the left-hand seat of an airplane."

To Kelsey, as to many Western ranchers, Texas Longhorns are a symbol of the old West, to be admired not only for their survival over four centuries, but for their spectacular horns, which can measure five feet across, and for their hides, which come in various colors that resemble porcelain art. These rangy Andalusian cattle were brought to Mexico by Cortez in 1521 and introduced to what is now the southwestern United States by Coronado and Father Kino in 1540. The Longhorns thrived in the hot climate of southwest Texas and soon covered the wide, unfenced brush country. Rugged and vigorous though they were, the longhorns were not con-

The castration of a three-year-old stallion by, left to right, Ted Evanoika, Lee Evanoika, John Brittingham and veterinarian Jim Munn.

sidered "meat" until after the Civil War, when they were rounded up by the hundreds of thousands and shipped north and east to answer the demand for beef.

"After that," said Terry Kelsey, nailing a shoe in place on his gelding, "your English breeds came in and the Longhorns pretty much died out."

"I didn't know there was such a thing as Longhorns left," said Sid Kelsey who, like Terry, was raised in Montana. "I saw them once in the Denver zoo. As soon as he heard there were Longhorns for sale, we took a load of hay and traded it for one cow. We called her Black Barta and she was totally blind for seven years."

"Next we bought two steers for $265," Terry said. "Concho and Poncho. We insured them against being struck by lightning and that very night Concho got killed."

"We collected four hundred dollars from the insurance company," Sid said, "and thought we were rich. So we went out and bought old Wild Cow from the Wichita Wildlife Refuge, and in the meantime Barta had her first bull calf. I guess you'd say we got started in the Longhorn business with $265 and a load of hay."

Sixty Longhorns now roam the rolling pastures where the Kelseys have their ranch; they have attached affectionate names to these animals, which Sid Kelsey loves enough to cry over when one of them dies or is hurt. There are Sarah, Flower, Footloose Flossie, Guinevere, Magnolia, Sweetie, Sugar and Columbine; there is also a bull named Billy the Kid.

The grass roots people have put something into the land to make it theirs, not as a private, legal possession but as something indelible, a frail mark on a relentless land, something that says: *I lived here. I farmed here. I was.* There is a sense of real physical pain when something goes wrong. They rejoice as much at rainfall as at the birth of a baby, weep over the blizzard's dead animals as they would weep over a dead aunt. Being there every day is what matters, to watch what's happening. The greening up in spring. The first dark clouds rolling in to announce the summer rain. They watch the sky for signs of geese heading south in the fall and for the arrival of the red-winged blackbirds at the end of winter. There is importance in weather reports but not in the national news; there is something to be gained by the sight of a newborn calf and an eagle on the wing. There is endless time and space to free the mind. There is peace in sameness, consolation in chores done well; there is the freedom that isolation brings.

As much as twenty miles lie between ranch houses. Between towns, as much as fifty. All around are vastness and loneliness, tumbleweeds and dust, parched earth and the great bowl of clear blue sky. Isolation creates a bond between the people who live on the land, connects the miles between neighbors, emphasizes the difference between them and city people, who are judged for their inability to cope with space. On Sundays, friends and relatives come to visit after church, a ritual that has not changed much in a hundred years. In summer, there are fairs in every county, with women and children working for weeks beforehand to prepare their best examples of sewing, canning, baking and vegetable growing. Homespun rodeos feature "real" instead of "professional" cowboys; livestock shows are best when they

The National Anthem, played at the West's oldest rodeo, at Deer Trail, stirs a patriotic audience.

are the result of 4-H Club effort. For most of the year, the emphasis is on school athletic events, which usually take priority over academic achievement; indeed, most college scholarships are athletic ones.

Rural women say there is always something to do, always a way to feel needed. There are weddings to sew for, babies to knit for, funerals and farm auctions to cook for. When a funeral time comes, church women fix a big meal and

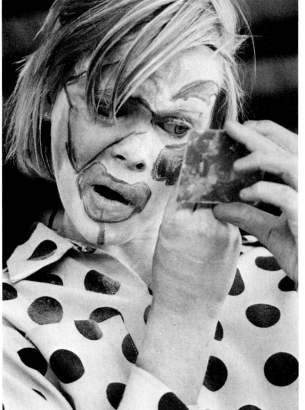

everyone comes, bringing more food than a family can eat in a week, and speaking more good words about the deceased than he could have deserved in one lifetime. Good neighbors. All of them. The grass roots people know one another. They have a commitment toward one another, toward God and work and family most of all. The rest of the nation does not seem to understand, but they are the root system that extends all across the land. There is as much pride in the face of a woman who has just put up fifteen hundred quarts of canned goods as there is in the surgeon who performs an operation to save a life. If rural women are not liberated, it is because they don't want to be. The greatest reward that life can give is to raise a healthy bunch of youngsters. What else can the

men do but appreciate them for that?

There is no more free land and no more un-spoiled frontier. The jets pass overhead on their way to New York and Los Angeles, and beer cans and piles of trash lie along the roads. Stop signs have been shot full of holes and fences cut for fun. In certain counties on the plains, there are widespread cattle mutilations, done at night by experts working out of helicopters, inflicting terror on the people, who sleep with guns be-neath their beds. One group of ranchers has of-fered a ten-thousand-dollar reward, but there

Opposite. *Grass roots women seem forged by land and the elements. Louise Foster, Elk Springs; Olive Gardner, Calhan, and Grace Tarpenning, Ramah. "My first husband got hit by a train, then my daughter got killed in a car wreck, and now my mother's had two heart attacks. But all in all, I'd say my life's been good."*

Above. *Rural teenagers enjoy moments of skill—and chivalry.*

are no clues and few leads. Most people believe it is a plot connected with the military, but others say that's what you get when outsiders start coming in.

There are no more wagon trains, but U-Hauls drive through, loaded down with the

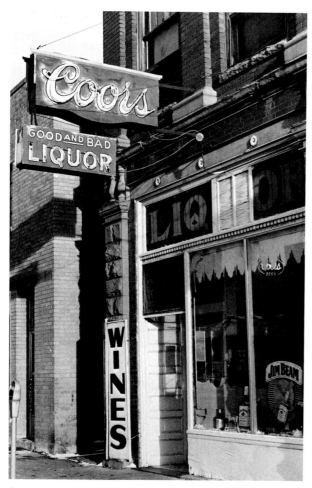

Main Street, Trinidad.

Lincoln County Fair, Hugo.

same sort of pioneer expectation. Yet the land's endurance is a façade—all over the plains, surveyors and geologists for the power companies have staked out the greatest strip-mining venture of all time. Coal is already being gouged out of the grasslands to provide power for the urban Midwest. Big-city claims on underground water tables will seriously threaten farms and ranches dependent on this supply for their wells and irrigation systems.

Still, no one is willing to acknowledge that

times are changing. Most prefer to look the other way when a small town dies or a new highway cuts through farmland. Outsiders are always mistrusted, whether they come from out of state with enough money to buy up the land or are city slickers seeking what it has taken the plains people generations to find out: You can only establish your roots through time. You belong here when your memory stops; when all you think of is knowing a place—its creeks and bluffs, its hills and gullies. The sound and smell

Spanish-American youth, Trinidad.

Mortician, Trinidad.

of it too. Who can describe the sensuousness of the first rain or the melancholy of the wind?

The grass roots people do not pretend to a poet's thoughts. They watch the sun come up, noticing its place upon the horizon, and whether it is farther north or south than it was the day before. They notice the rain walking out of a summer sky and think: Forty-hundredths of an inch if we're lucky—and pray in their own way for the cattle nibbling the parched grass or for the wheat withering in the fields.

The generation who wore out as the land wore in are in their old age now, afflicted as much by nostalgia as by the arthritis that has bent their plow fingers into a permanent curl. They like to tell their stories to anyone who will listen, gaining recognition from the fact that what they remember best is what the world has forgotten most—who really cares about kerosene tractors and horse-drawn buggies anymore? Such a life sounds obsolete, if not irrelevant, and that's what worries them most: they

*Billy Copp watches as his grandmother, Agnes Copp, left,
weighs a canteloupe at the Cheat 'Em and Chisel 'Em Market,
Pueblo. Owner Frank Martino muses: "On the Fourth of July
in '47 I sold 90,000 pounds of watermelon in one weekend.
Stacked 20,000 pounds of ice on top of it. I even made 'Believe
It or Not.' But now I just want to sell out."*

have spent a lifetime on the land and nobody
seems to care except the oral-history students
who come out with tape recorders and expres-
sions of high esteem.

Rawboned, perpetually restless, united by
memories that have forgotten the bad, the old-
timers are the last generation to have done it
themselves forty or fifty years ago when land
was cheap (ten dollars an acre), labor was plen-
tiful (fifty dollars a month—ten dollars more if
you broke horses and put up hay) and farm and
cattle markets were steady. Change is coming in
a way they don't understand. Not only are economics squeezing them out, but progress is
boxing them in. With their horizon already
shortened by automobiles, their backyard
claimed by real estate developers wanting to sell
ten-acre "ranchettes" and by city dwellers willing to commute an hour or more to live out
there, their familiar world is going by as fast as
the noon *Zephyr* which used to fly past on the
railroad tracks. Small towns wither because the
current generation does not want to live without
the cultural and social opportunities they have
come to expect. Farms dissolve when real estate
developers step in. Ranches disappear when
taxes get too high. To this older generation,
progress means defeat.

Most of these old-timers are the descendants
of those who answered the call "Go West," and
went. To an inhospitable land where familiar

crops would not grow. To a climate so dry that it
cracked the skin of the women and turned them
old before their time. To a future that held but
one certainty—uncertainty. Most of the home-
steaders of the last century who started out
turned back. Others went bust on the sorry land
that was given them for nothing, and drifted
away to the cities to find jobs. Those who
stayed, struggled on little farms and ranches. It
was not feasible to ranch or farm only 160 acres,
so if they did not go broke, they added to their
stake a little bit at a time. If a man died with a
section (640 acres) to his name, he considered
himself rich.

And there were compensations for the hard
life. In children and in neighbors. In gardens
and "handwork," as the women used to call it.
For the men, the reward would come later,
when the next generation elected to take over
the family ranch and the land that had so much
effort spent upon it. It is this generation that
must decide who gets the farm when the
parents die or, given all the work, who will *want*
the farm when the parents die. There are other
questions too. Will inheritance taxes make it
impossible to keep the same name on the barn
another generation? Is it better to incorporate?
And with the government controlling farm
prices and practices more and more, will it ever
pay to plant? Old men, who want to pass on
nothing more than their hard-earned wisdom,
find it is a commodity that's nearly obsolete.
The plow that broke the plains is broken now itself.

But for John Mikita, retired to a comfortable
house now at sixty-nine, the reward is in turn-

ing over his small farm near Ramah to his oldest son, Larry. He worked nearly fifty years to put together seven hundred acres of fertile land along Big Sandy Creek, which runs dry most of the year. One Eastern Orthodox Easter, John Mikita and his wife, Mildred, came up from their "city" house in Calhan to have dinner with their son Larry and his wife, Darlene, and their three children. Sitting on the couch and sipping a little whiskey, John Mikita said:

"My father came from Czechoslovakia in 1906 and homesteaded 160 acres, then bought another quarter section. We had no pleasures to speak of, but then we didn't need any. We raised beans, corn, wheat, oats and barley. We'd trade for eggs and cream and at Christmas we sold turkeys. Mikita's turkeys were known as the best around. Mildred and I got married in '29 and times were tough. We were never rich but we had plenty to eat, even in the Depression. Except once. We were out working in the fields and some drunkards came by and ate the bread and ate the bacon—raw, with some salt and pepper on it. You could eat it raw because we cured it six or seven weeks in that smokehouse out back. She said, 'The bread's gone,' and I said, 'You've got flour, ain't you?' "

After the fact, laughter eases the harshness of past events, creates a legend out of what everyone expects such a generation to stand for. And that is what they pass on. The words of the grass roots people form an unconscious obituary for a life they are still trying to define.

Still in their Easter clothes, John and Mildred Mikita went outside and stood in the harsh wind in front of the place where they used to

Mildred Mikita, Ramah, relaxes with her grandchildren. "Without these kids I'd be old or dead."
John and Mildred Mikita in front of the dugout where they lived for thirty years. "Retired is a bad thing. It means you can't get up at five o'clock the way you used to."

live. Mildred hung on to John as if to anchor him to the ground and said:

"For thirty years we lived in this old dugout, thirty-six by thirty-six, half in and half out of the ground. It was warm in winter and cool in summer. We only moved out in '75. The walls were cracking and snakes were coming in. It's still a good house, though, if a person wanted to fix it up."

And she walked through the old dugout, remembering how, living beneath the ground, she was only able to see the bottoms of things. She got to recognize people by their legs coming up to the door and to gauge the weather by how fast the weeds were blowing past.

The family sat down to a table richly laden with food, standing first to give thanks for the food and for their families, for their neighbors and the good that had come to them in the past year. At one end of the table sat Annette Trojanovitch, the mother of Darlene Mikita. For thirty years Annette and her husband, Mike, farmed across the road from the Mikitas. But fate turned against the Trojanovitches. Carefully cutting her meat, Annette said:

"When I came on that farm in '28, straight out of Chicago, I didn't know much about farms, but I learned. Milking cows, butchering hogs, making soap, churning butter, and when I wasn't having babies, helping out in the fields.

"We were making out fine and then the De-

Annette Trojanovitch used to ranch with her husband, but has had to work in a food-processing plant since his death. "We got used to making do."

Like a farmer, he was going to keep a-working, but cancer got to his arm. He died in '61. Up until he got sick we had been free and clear of debt. But he was so long in the hospital that I had to sell the farm to pay the bills. I went to work in town, at a factory that makes Mexican food. Oh, it's not so bad. You should see my family now. I have nineteen grandchildren and two great-grandchildren."

Annette Trojanovitch looked down the long table, where some of her grandchildren were eating. She had paid the price. If she had expected something better, she kept it to herself. The plains did that to women, made them bear up and in the process gave them the elements of an existential life. Time had not charged reality against her, but it had written endurance across her face.

"All in all, it worked out fine," Annette Trojanovitch said, and everyone believed her.

Vernon is in the middle of Yuma County, on a flat, dusty back road that leads off into the parched wheat fields that stretch for fifty miles or more. Yuma County was among those worst hit by the March blizzard; over ninety percent of the farmers in that county alone had to borrow in order to start farming in the spring. Even then, the money did not bring moisture. Wheat farmers watched their fields blow away, the topsoil rising before their eyes until the whole horizon was full and throbbing, an ominous black in the middle of the day. In the once fertile Arikaree valley, old wells started running dry and the river itself was heavy with dust for the first time in twenty years. All over Yuma County,

pression came. It nearly wiped us out. We went to the Farmers' Bank there in Calhan to borrow a hundred dollars just to stay alive. They said all right, but what we had to put up was the land, the cows, fifteen chickens, the house and all the household goods, and the only team of horses we had.

"We finally got on our feet and were doing good when in '57 he got pulled into a hay baler.

Herbert Dickson, wheat farmer, Vernon. "A drought like this turns neighbor against neighbor."

farmers started "coloring" their water, an act that implied both desperation and mistrust.

"It's a terrible thing to do to a fellow you've known all your life," said Herbert Dickson, a wheat farmer from Vernon. "But if it's his survival or your survival, well, water comes before friendship out here. If you think your neighbor is taking your water, you have a right to put color in your well. The law says you can do it and you got to or else starve out. If the color turns up in his water, it proves he's taking it." He considered the complications of a life that had once been so simple. "Of course the other fellow can do it to you, too."

Forty years ago, Vernon used to be a center for farmers and ranchers who lived nearby, but now, in trucks and cars, they speed past the sleepy little town, population thirty, toward Wray and Burlington. There is no need for Vernon to exist, but it does anyway, a sun-bleached

past-tense town made up mostly of deserted buildings, an empty town square and half a dozen families who stay because they've always been there. The schoolhouse has been closed for years, but just before Mother's Day each year the women around Vernon come in and clean it up for an annual tea.

The Vernon post office is in a false-fronted old wooden building with a faded sign that does not even have the zip code on it. All it says is VERNON, in hand-painted letters six inches high. Blanche DeVore has been postmistress there since 1951 and in the course of time has rearranged the post office to suit herself. The front part of it is a public library consisting of a ten-foot shelf of old books that people have brought in, adventure and mystery stories, for the most part, with a generous selection of Reader's Digest Condensed Books thrown in. There is a reading table and a neat pile of maga-

50

zines. The library runs into the grocery store, where a shelf of *Reader's Digest*s and *National Geographic*s joins a shelf of tissue, canned milk and Campbell's soup. Where the grocery plays out, the post office begins—a grilled window and a row of mailboxes. Opposite Blanche De-Vore's library and grocery store wall, there is a quick-lunch counter, where townspeople can stop for a cup of coffee and a sandwich.

"People don't come in just for mail," Blanche DeVore said, stepping out of her post office long enough to rearrange the green plants that were growing in the library. "They stop in here because we're in the center of things."

When the blizzard hit in March, the post office closed for a day and a half and Blanche De-Vore set up a soup kitchen behind the mailboxes, where she usually cooks a noon meal for herself and her husband, Harold. During the blizzard, when the post office became a check point for ranchers searching for lost cattle, Blanche kept a lost-and-found sheet going on the reading table.

"The roads were closed and all the telephone poles were snapped off like matchsticks," she said. "A lot of the ranchers came in on snowmobiles and sat around waiting for their cattle to turn up. The electricity was off, but I cooked on that gas stove back there and we got out the kerosene lamps and just waited. People who hadn't seen each other for months sat around and talked and comforted each other. It was good to know you could come in here and get warm, have something hot to eat, and find out if your neighbor was worse off than you. A terrible time, but it sort of brought people to-

gether, you know what I mean?"

Finished selling a loaf of bread and a package of lunch meat to a wetback who spoke no English, Blanche DeVore went back to sorting the mail.

"I guess this post office is just a place for people to come in and find out what's going on in the world."

But the world she means is the world of Vernon and the world of Vernon is seen differently by different people. Harold DeVore stopped the minor repair job he was doing in the post office and went outside. He walked along the empty street with the dust blowing up in his face and looked around the town where he has lived all his life. What he saw was not really the emptiness, or the obvious marks of a town coming to its natural end.

"Over there is where the bank stood," Harold DeVore said, and he saw clearly what Vernon was in its day. "And on that corner was the drugstore, with a movie house on top. There were five churches at one time and a doctor's office and a barbershop right there. We had two grocery stores and a livery stable. We even had a brass band once. We had two hotels and five stores where you could buy most anything, just like a city. We had a pool hall too, but liquor was never allowed in our town. A fellow tried to open a saloon one fall and they had him out before his rent fell due."

Until a heart attack laid him up a few years ago, Harold DeVore ran a gas station and a ma-

Harold DeVore, Vernon's jack-of-all-trades. "There's going to come a time when there won't be a demand for men like me."

chine shop. He could fix anything, Harold De-Vore could, because he was good with his hands and he never threw anything away. His shop is filled with mechanical objects he has collected over the years, and when he touches the grimy parts of engines even now, his hands make the same quick assessment that they always did. The old gasoline pumps are gone, but in his shop Harold DeVore still fixes things,

still gives out advice on how to make a carbu-retor work or what to do when a bearing goes out.

"There's going to come a time when there won't be a need for men like me," he said, and pondered the truth of it. "I hired two fellows when I was sick. They didn't do anything except want to get paid, so I told them to go back to town. I'll do it myself," I said.

"In the Depression, I learned how to make use of everything. In those days you had to. There never was a piece of wire or a nut or a bolt that I didn't hang on to. We had to make do. That's all it was—making do."

But for Harold DeVore, life in Vernon meant other things too.

"For me the best thing about living here was that I got to help people. There wasn't a rig I couldn't fix or a fellow I didn't like—and no-body who didn't pay."

He stopped and summed up his whole ca-reer.

"I was an honest man and I worked hard all my life."

For the grass roots people, those two attri-butes are the most important ones there are. They also have a strong allegiance to the nation, especially when conservatives are running it and "government interference" seems less. If they resent anything, it is being told what to do; if they share common dislikes, it is for hippies, welfare, laziness, communists, atheists, draft dodgers, labor unions, minorities, women's lib-eration, "snot-nosed college kids" and any kind of government regulation. Ironically, it was the government they appealed to for support in their desperate American Agriculture strike. Rural people are a stubborn, hard-working lot who expect no less of others than they do of themselves; they work to keep from idleness and their greatest return is in knowing that their neighbors think well of them. Churchgoing, God-fearing and often verging on self-righteousness, they prefer to cling to what they're used to rather than risk a change. In a rural society of thin phone books, the grass roots people know everyone listed in their own exchange and believe themselves to be the better for it.

"You do better than you think you can, then you run the risk of people saying, There goes a man who does better than he ought to."

"Never mind what other folks think. Just get up in the morning and do what you got to."

"But like I said, we got used to waiting. We waited for school to end so vacation could begin. We waited for vacation to end so we could wait for it to begin again. We waited for things to change. When they didn't change, a lot of people moved away. Them that stayed still wait, out of habit mostly."

Not far from Vernon, an old rancher and his wife opened the windows of their sod house and began to sweep out the dust that had accumulated over the winter.

"We live in Wray during the winter," Bob Jones said, "but when the grass begins to grow I got to get out where it's at." The sun, poised just above the horizon, streamed in the windows and spilled across the carpeted floor. Bea Jones came out of the bedroom, a small, gentle woman with the steady assurance of one who knows another human being completely. She

Robert and Bea Jones, Wray. "She says she's old and can't do anything anymore, but the other day she made eleven pies."

has been sixty years a wife, ever since she was sixteen years old.

"I don't remember anything else," she said, and put the coffee on. "I wouldn't *want* to remember anything else."

Eight children too, she said, and began to tell what it was like to raise them on a ranch. It all went by so fast. And now?

"I have a contented mind," Bea Jones said.

Three generations of Jones men have farmed the same land near Wray for forty years.

"I can tell you it's worth more than all the money in the world." She moved gracefully about the small, tidy kitchen, rubbing her finger on top of the refrigerator to see if she had gotten the dust.

"She says she's old and can't do anything anymore," Bob Jones said, "but the other day she made eleven pies." With his gold teeth shining, he looked at her in the way that comes

after so much living together that you know each other's thoughts.

Bob Jones has eight thousand acres which he has worked all his life to accumulate. He raises corn, alfalfa, wheat and cattle, and he has not been much affected by the drought because of an expensive irrigation system. "Whatever that new well cost, it was worth it," Bob Jones said. "Now I can drink the coffee without chewin' it."

Out on the land, he was given to history, to what he was able to do during his lifetime, to what he hoped his son and grandson would continue to do long after he was gone. "Oh, it'll continue. It *has* to continue. There is some of me in every mile of fence. There is some of me in that corn field over there. When a man works all his life to build a thing like this, well, it's darn sure the closest thing to immortality he's going to come to."

He stopped to get his facts straight. "I was born in Hartley, Nebraska, in '98. My father came from Missouri and he lived in a sod house first. When he went to build his first frame house, right after he and Mother were married, corn was selling for eight cents a bushel. Mother wanted him to wait, but he sold his corn so he would know how big a house he could build. He sold three thousand bushels and built three rooms. In May, corn was thirty-five cents a bushel. He could have had a house four times bigger.

"Bea and I were married in Nebraska, then went to Kansas in '23. Stayed there until '37, when things were so bad I saw thistles growing out of the backs of cattle from all the dust. We

National Western Stock Show, Denver, is the annual highlight of stock growers throughout the West.

came here to this country and bought a half section for two-twenty an acre and then three and a half sections for five dollars an acre. I bought it for a thousand dollars down and a handshake on the rest. It's the way business is still done between ranchers. I've seen million-dollar deals closed with nothing but a handshake. It's a man's word, you see. He has to live up to it all his life. If a man's word gets to be no good, you know his money isn't worth much either.

"Oh, but it was rough in the dirty thirties. For light, we used a basket of cobs and a quart of kerosene. I saw twelve-cent corn and twenty-five-cent wheat. But we didn't have to take relief and we didn't go hungry. We raised enough to eat and buy clothes.

"Nobody asked but what we'd help 'em. Sometimes they didn't help us, but when they'd ask, we'd help.

"You can't buy friendship and you can't buy neighbors. If a fellow doesn't have neighbors, you know the reason why."

Turning his face to the sun, Bob Jones said: "The kind of life I'm telling you about is mostly through. It was a time of trust. You left the door unlocked. You never made a dime off the other fellow's hard luck. You had to be good neighbors with one another. You picked a good woman for a wife.

"And that," he concluded, "is what I call the essential facts of life."

Every January, when the weather is coldest, a phenomenon hits Denver that is second only to the mania that sweeps the city whenever its football team, the Denver Broncos, is playing in Mile High Stadium. For seventy-three years, the National Western Stock Show has been playing to capacity crowds in the chilly, dusty Denver Coliseum. For ten straight days, livestock, rang-

National Western Stock Show activities include warm water baths and blow drying for cattle; a free foot massage for the ladies; and a chance to perform in the Coliseum for young girl members of the Westernaires.

ing all the way from combed and curried prize bulls to poultry and rabbits, is brought out and judged on conformation and on appearance, an attribute that requires hours of preparation.

In the Bovine Beauty Salon, next to the arena, cattle are first shampooed with warm water, then blown dry. After that, their hair is combed and teased until it stands up, as soft

and smooth as plush carpet. Even their tails are not overlooked. Prior to judging, stock owners will spend hours teasing the tips of cattle tails into a giant tumbleweed, which is then encased in a hairnet. Black Angus cattle receive even more attention: any hairs that are not black are spray-painted that color; their hoofs are laboriously lacquered with black shoe polish. But the obsession with color once proved embarrassing to stock-show officials who declared a Black Angus steer grand champion only

to have his color wash off, revealing a beige-colored Charolais underneath.

Professional groomers may attend to the beautification of the cattle, but more often it is the owners themselves, who can have as much as sixteen thousand dollars riding on whether their entry is declared grand champion or not. So important is appearance that an exhibitor will often stand, pitchfork in hand, behind the animal's rump, in order to catch the prodigious excrement that would otherwise discolor its immaculate hide.

But for most cattlemen, the stock show offers something else—a yearly chance to talk to other producers from all over the country and to view the latest in ranch machinery and gadgets on display in the exhibition hall. Cattle sales generally offer an indication of what the livestock market will be like for the rest of the year, reason enough for cattlemen to stay up all night speculating on how much their animals will bring at the next day's auction.

Stock-show time also means one of the most dazzling rodeos put on in the West, complete with the famous Budweiser Clydesdale team and an all-girl group of precision riders known as the Westernaires. For kids, the stock show means the day of reckoning, when their year-long efforts with 4-H Club calves and sheep are judged just as severely as those of their grown-up counterparts.

Every spring when the weather begins to warm and the flowers start pushing up through the brown grass in the fields, the Thunderbird Extension Club cleans the Simla cemetery. For

Top left. *4-H Club members spend hours grooming animals for judging.*
Bottom left. *The John Birch Society hands out literature at the National Western Stock Show.*
Above. *Rancher George Young, Simla.*

thirty-five years the women have been coming with rakes and shovels and cleaning out the trash and dead leaves so that at the end of the day, the cemetery is as good as new. And every year, for nearly as long, a rancher named George Young comes with them and sits on a tombstone, waiting for them to finish their work. At noon, George Young, who is eighty-five years old, takes the women of the Thunderbird Extension Club to a lunch put on by the VFW Auxiliary at the Simla Community Hall. Most of George Young's family is in the Simla cemetery and perhaps it is to spend the day near them that he comes. One morning in early May, George Young sat on the edge of a cemetery plot and said:

"I have the oldest registered Hereford herd owned by one owner in the state of Colorado. I have had it since 1918 and that's almost sixty years now. I've been a rancher all my life. I was born in Washington County in a sod house and moved here when I was six or so. We ranched and farmed and broke horses and did everything it was honorable to do. I was married fifty-eight years, but she died of cancer three years ago. I had a son die of a blood clot when he was only forty-two. I lost another son in the flood of '65, trying to save his greyhounds. A wall of water eight feet high came down the creek bed while he was between the house and the kennels. I saw it coming over at my place and I never thought he'd be out in it, that he wouldn't hear it coming. It made such a terrible noise. Well, it was the next day before we found him, swept up along the fence line. I just picked him up and carried him into the house and my wife cleaned him up. The phones were out and the roads were closed and we just sat there for two days waiting for the undertaker to come. People say I've had a hard life, but I know those who have had it worse. I've always believed a man should not complain."

With that, George Young got up, tightened his bola tie and gathered up his cemetery clean-

ers. It was time for lunch and the old rancher would not be late.

"A man that lacks courage don't come out here."

"If you can lick this land, you can lick anything."

"Out here they say a man can grow as big as the country. I can't help but think the land makes his thoughts grow too."

"They put a plow to this country and it blowed away. They put cattle on it and it shriveled up. They tried corn and harvested dust. Do you know what this country's good for? I reckon it's good for itself."

VALLEYS

The Mora River is not much as rivers go. Sluggish, half-hearted and of timid disposition, it escapes from the Sangre de Cristo Mountains near Chacon and joins the Canadian River in the splotchy red desert above Sabinoso. Along the way, the river gnaws through a hundred miles of farm and ranch land, some of it occupied continuously since the Spanish began to work the reluctant soil early in the nineteenth century.

Once, when it was carefully tended, the land yielded. One by one, the rocks were cleared from the fields and made into walls. Water borrowed from the river ran in ditches all across the desert, forcing it to bloom. Bare shoulders lassoed to a plow coaxed the soil; bare hands thinned the crops, pulled the weeds, gathered up the harvest. But most of the little farms are gone now, the farmers laid to rest in back-road graveyards, their headstones, carved in Spanish, so old that no one has insulted them with the ubiquitous plastic flowers. Crumbling haciendas bake beneath the sun—adobe tombstones in fields of creeping sage and cactus.

The river is not running anymore, but at night the old ones listen. There was once a *caballero* from one of the big ranches who used to ride up it, looking for his drowned sweetheart, they say. You could hear him clattering over the big rocks, calling her name in the dark. *Luisa.* Now, when the wind is right, you can still hear him, the name drawn out into three long syllables. *Loo-eees-sah!*

The river. Filled with mystery, if not water; sanctified by axles, wheels and hub caps, bald tires and car chassis, washing machines with legs and chairs with broken arms. In the old days, when crucifixion was still permitted, the Penitentes stopped along the river and washed the Cristo's wounds. In these places the river is still sacred; the mud from it will cure headaches and arthritis, bring on an overdue baby or make a weak heart strong.

Or so the old ones say.

Time has afforded them the misspent luxury of applying past to present; here are dialects last heard in Spain in the seventeenth century; here are *brujas* with their evil spells; here, too, old Penitentes with worn-out knees shuffling into windowless *moradas* during Holy Week, the heavy wooden crosses they used to carry forgotten, along with the *sangrador,* who used to cut herringbone patterns into their backs with a razor-sharp knife.

The people do not like to be reminded of those solemn rituals of atonement, so misunderstood and sensationalized in the press. A man's penance is between himself and God, they say. Perhaps there is still physical pain involved; perhaps not. For the people of the valley, pain is as daily as tortillas and beans. And religion, like politics, is best when kept unseen.

Along this river and across this valley, the people do not like to be called Chicano. "Chicano" has radical overtones, they say, implying boycotts, hunger strikes and class action suits against your enemies. Better to live quietly and simply, close to family and to neighbors, even if you shoot them sometimes. Better to be close to God, even when you are drunk and the food stamps do not come in. One must not become

involved, even when there are no jobs.

On Saturdays the Spanish people around Watrous go for wood, as far as to the Sangre de Cristo Mountains, fifty miles west. It used to be possible for them to gather wood where the Mora and Sapello rivers come together, in the rich bottom lands where the cottonwoods have grown thick and tall; but recently the new owners of the big ranches came in and put locks on all the gates going into the bottom lands. The people around Watrous who need wood for heat and cooking have met the change in various ways.

On a side street in Watrous, population fifty, a somber-eyed young man swung an ax one warm, dry winter day, his tattooed forearm hard with muscle. A miraculous medal dangled from his bare neck, along with a string of beads. His real name was Leroy Garcia, but everyone called him Doy. He was twenty-seven years old and he had always lived in this little hamlet just east of I-25, in the same two-room adobe house with his father, Lorenzo, who raised him after his mother died. Now Doy Garcia had a wife, sixteen years old, who watched him through the window while he chopped the wood into pieces small enough to fit into the stove. The three of them lived in the house together, the old man sleeping in a small room next to the young couple.

"Sometimes I think about buying a trailer and moving to Albuquerque, where there is more work," he said solemnly. But he could not leave the old man, who had retired a few years before from the Santa Fe Railroad. What would he do in Albuquerque, away from everyone he

Top left. *The San Luis valley near Las Sauses, Colorado.*
Bottom left. *The people of Watrous have had to chop down their trees to ensure a winter firewood supply.*
Above. *Denise and Leroy Garcia, Watrous.*

knew? "No," Doy Garcia said, "we will not go to Albuquerque just yet."

The ax came down heavily, as if to make his point, and split the log in two. It was still a little green, but that could not be helped. When winter began, Doy Garcia had to cut down all the big cottonwood trees that used to stand in front of his father's house. The trees were old

Denise Garcia peers through her window while her cat dozes in the sun.

quiet, regal bearing even when she was making flour tortillas in the kitchen, her small hands shaping the dough into little balls which were rolled out flat and smooth before she dropped them on the hot skillet. Every day Denise Garcia made flour tortillas and swept the house clean as a whistle. There was no heat except for the wood stove, no water except what Doy carried from the shallow well behind the house, no plumbing except for a privy in the back. There was no television; only a radio that stayed tuned to a Spanish-speaking station. At night the three of them sat around the table and listened to it, played cards and talked. There was always something to talk about.

Now the talk was mainly about the baby who was coming in two months. Denise said that the baby was going to be a boy and she would call it Leroy, after her husband. The baby had been paid for already, $375 saved up over the last six months and paid to the hospital in Las Vegas, twenty miles south. The doctor was free at the clinic. The next thing was to save for a car. The old one was too old; a new one cost too much. Still, in a year they could have a down payment. Every two weeks Doy brought home $170 from his job at an old folks' home in Las Vegas.

"It's enough to get by on," he said, lifting a pail of water onto the stove. "Maybe next year, when these trees are all burned up, it will also be enough to buy wood."

Marcelena Arroyos slipped out of the trees like a cat, stopped, and looked around. The day had turned cold and snow was hanging in the

and they shaded the house in summer and kept the winter winds from coming through the cracks. Up on the hill, across the railroad tracks, Doy's father-in-law, Joe Sanchez, has had to cut down his trees too.

"It's too much trouble to go all the way to the mountains anymore," Doy said with a shrug, gathering up the wood he had chopped. "It costs too much for gas."

Denise Garcia had the face of a madonna, a

Marcelena Arroyos stands in her kitchen crowded with forty years of living.

ashen sky to the north. Before morning, the ground would all be white. That meant she would have to get another load of wood before the pale sun sank behind the mountains. She had waited too long and now there was no wood at home, just the big log she was rolling down the hill by herself and the wagonload of kindling she pulled along. She wrapped her ragged coat around her and said in Spanish, "That's what happens sometimes when you do not plan ahead. I should have known the storm was coming. It is winter, after all." She gave the log a kick and watched it roll down the hill.

Marcelena dumped the kindling behind her house, then went back for the log lying at the bottom of the hill, breathing hard from so much effort. After her husband died many years ago, she had grown used to hauling wood alone, out of the piñon forest a mile or so away. "If you help me it will not be good," she said. "I will

become spoiled and lazy. I will forget how to work when there is no one else around."

A pickup rattled past. An Anglo was driving and he waved stiffly but did not smile. The brand inspector, who lives down the road, she explained. Marcelena's husband used to work for him, doing odd jobs. He got perhaps five, six dollars a day. One time, after he died, she asked the brand inspector to get her some wood.

"The Anglos do not tell you no," she said. "They just tell you there is no time." She watched him disappear around a bend in the road, then began to shove the log toward home. "Anglos do not want to stoop over," she said. "We Mexicans were born that way."

She laughed at the truth of it, successful in her resistance to anger and despair.

Marcelena's tiny adobe house was cluttered with what she had managed to save over forty

Marcelena Arroyos wraps up against the winter cold as she sets out for firewood.

picture of Nuestra Señora, to be kissed when she was finished praying, and a crucifix made of wood, to be placed under the pillow when there was sickness or danger from the *bruja*'s evil spell. There were votive candles to be lighted to the memory of her husband and of relatives gone so long their names seemed strange to the tongue. And a *rosario*, the beads worn smooth from passing through her fingers so many times. This was a house where praying seemed to have hallowed the walls; it was a place where sacred repetition dispelled unholy fear. All was ritual and benediction in Marcelena Arroyos' house.

She called to her dog in Spanish and he got up from his heap of rags and pulled off her canvas gloves gently, so not to bite through the thin cloth to her fingers. Her hands were as smooth as polished wood, with the heavy grain of hardship worn into them; the straining muscles and aging bones had formed a knotted landscape under the tobacco-colored skin.

"There are many uses for the fat of a wolf," she said, shoving kindling into the old iron stove. "You should try some on your hands." The room was cold but it warmed quickly, and the stove cast a pleasant glow on the sooty walls. It was only recently that she had got the wringer washer that stood in one corner, covered with blankets. The water had to be hauled, one bucket at a time, from the well in the back, then heated on the stove. It took all day to wash clothes that way, she said. But they came out cleaner. Unless they fell apart in the machine.

She made coffee, went out and fed the chick-

years in the same place. There was only a small space to sit, on a bench shoved up against a table covered with open cans of food, grain for the chickens and heaps of ragged clothing. On the wall was a 1962 calendar with a picture of Pope Paul. She kept it because she liked the picture. "The Pope is a kind man," she said. "Why else would he be father to so many people?"

On a shelf in the corner, Marcelena had the symbols of her religion laid out. There was a

ens, told the dog to carry the empty grain can inside, then chopped up the wood in the yard, swinging the ax with long, deliberate strokes that had become precise from so much practice. By the time she was finished, it was dark and snowing hard.

"The wood will last three days," she said, carrying an armload through the door. "Three days is enough to think about at one time." The dog nodded his head in agreement, then lay at her feet while she put some beans on the stove to cook, adding a dash of cumin to the layer of grease that had congealed on the top.

In three days' time Marcelena Arroyos would go again into the piñon forest. Perhaps she would find wood then. Perhaps not. The snow could be very deep. She had learned not to worry about it.

"God will provide even wood," she said.

There is no name on the outside of the old adobe cantina in Ocaté, population sixty-two, a mile or so down the road from the post office, only the bent metal frame of a Falstaff beer sign that was shot out one night by some teen-agers driving past. Except for the cantina, there is no place to go. The young ones drag-race up and down the highway, twenty-three miles to Wagon Mound, eighteen miles to Black Lake, but the road isn't paved and the cars rattle past in the night. Nine miles to Ojo Feliz. Thirteen to Romeroville. Nineteen to La Cueva. Back and forth they go, caught in this place they have come to hate, hesitant to go too far, loath to stay where they are.

Joe Lucero stood smoking a cigarette behind the bar, next to a sign that advised: "Buy Victory Bonds." The room was small and dim; it smelled of stale beer and the heavy sweat of the bar customers. The room was bare except for a pool table, a jukebox and three sacks of pinto beans, sold by the pound to the neighbors passing by. There were only a dozen half-empty bottles of liquor to choose from, most of it tequila and cheap bourbon. Joe had been running the cantina for four months.

"The first month, I shot a man in the leg," he announced. "A nineteen-year-old kid." He blew the smoke in a perfect ring. "He hit me in the head with a cue ball first."

Joe Lucero had the broken cue ball stored in a box. He took it out and held a piece in each hand insisting it had been broken over his head.

"I shot him in the leg. Oh, I could have gone for his nuts, but I didn't. A troublemaker. No, the police didn't come. Why should they come? They're twenty-five miles away."

And it was clear that the police belonged where they were and Joe Lucero belonged where he was. Almost.

The people around Ocaté were angry with Joe Lucero, partly because of the shooting, partly because he had come from Mora, a couple of hills away, and was therefore considered an outsider until he proved himself to be otherwise. There was a rumor that someone wanted to kill him, so he kept two loaded guns behind the bar—a .38 revolver and a .22 magnum rifle, the one he shot the kid with. He slept on a cot in a corner of the bar, next to the gas stove, but never more than five hours a night. He was too restless to sleep much, but said it was because

of an old injury he got when he worked in a uranium mine. Joe Lucero had mined coal and copper too. But since he got hurt, he had had to run a bar, the last one, prior to Ocaté, in Mora, where his family still lived.

He went over to the cot and sat down, pulling another .38 from beneath his pillow.

"You have to be ready for anything here," he said, spinning the chamber of the gun. There were six bullets in it. "You can't give anybody a second chance or they will kill you." His fingers closed around it like an old friend.

"Enough of that," he said, putting the gun away. "I am also a poet. I will give you one of my poems, if you like."

From the box where he kept the broken cue ball he took out a sheet of lined paper. On it was written:

When I and my love
May leave in each of our hearts
I to the silent grave must go
Sleep and weep as others do.
With meditation read these lines
You may in them a secret find.
All this and more I could say but
Nite calls and I must obey.

"There is a question in this poem," Joe Lucero said politely. "Do you know what the question is? Well, it is the first word in each line: 'When may I sleep with you all night?' "

Fecundo Archuleta's adobe house rises on a stone foundation from a bare dirt yard six miles west of Watrous, where the cottonwoods grow along a bend in the Mora River. He stood before it, a long-legged, sinewy man whose marble-

Top left. *The Mora River valley near Ocaté, New Mexico.*
Bottom left. *Joe Lucero, Ocaté. He keeps three guns in his bar.*
Above. *Margarito Vigil, Ocaté.*

shaped eyes roamed the familiar landscape about him—the windmill with its blades moving clockwise, drawing the water out of the ground; the wire fence held up with juniper staves that he had cut himself over half a century ago; the old tractor parked where he left it months before; the shovel with a wooden handle sticking out of a manure pile; a bucket

He cannot add, but Fecundo Archuleta knows how many sheep he has and how many geese are flying overhead.

hung up on a fence post; a wagon wheel discarded in the middle of the yard. Behind him, wedged up against a cliff, its windows broken out, was a school bus. No one lived in the bus, but he liked to have it there, a jaunty blue amid what was earth-colored or bleached or worn out.

Fecundo Archuleta's one-room house was clean and spare, with a thin film of dust over everything. He stirred the air as he bent to light the kerosene lamp, scraping a match across the seat of his pants. The light flickered into cobwebbed corners, coated the dirt floor, evoked a past as old as the back of his work-worn hands. He sat on the narrow bed, which sagged under his weight. For covers he used two gunnysacks and a tarp; for a pillow a flour sack filled with sheep's wool.

"No, señora, I have no wife," he said softly in Spanish. "I never found the right woman. I am still looking for her. There is still time. There is still a possibility, no?" But it was not so much a question as an evaluation of remaining opportunity.

He looked up at the low ceiling. It was covered with old *Playboy* magazines which he had put there for insulation. "Out here the winters are very cold," he said. "The wind cries like a baby at night. The cold seeps in through the walls unless you are careful. In this house there are no cracks. There is only good adobe, warm in winter, cool in summer. The wind tries to put holes in the adobe. So you are always taking care of a house like you take care of a woman. Dust still comes in, though, and there is not a crack anywhere. Who knows why?"

The mystery of the dust eluded him; he blew a cloud of it off the old dresser and watched it settle on his bedroom slippers. "Come," he said abruptly, and put on his worn felt hat.

Fecundo Archuleta moved across the frozen earth in long, graceful strides, his fine, distant eyes watching a flock of Canadian geese coming in for the night. *"Catorce."* He had never learned to count, but he knew how many geese there were. He could not tell time, but he always knew what time it was. He did not know how to read a calendar either, but he never missed the first day of deer season. He was said to be the best shot in Mora County, the first to get a deer when the season opened.

"Ovejas. Ovejas." He called to the sheep grazing out of sight among the cottonwoods, indistinct in the fading light. They heard him and came running, crowding around him to eat the feed he dumped on the ground.

He said he had been robbed four days before. He was gone for a little while and somebody came and stole all his guns and hunting knives. Somebody had been after him for a while now. One night while he slept, they tried to break in. He fired through the door in the dark with a thirty aught six, his deer-hunting gun. It left a hole. "You should see the hole I covered with a coffee lid," he said. "But the *cabrón* who tried to break in, he does not have a hole in him yet. Soon he will have a hole right here in the stomach."

He grabbed the front of his shirt to show where the bullet hole would go.

At seventy-four, he still fought. Sometimes he fought so hard that he had to go to the doctor to get sewed up.

"If it were not for the doctor, I could not fight," Fecundo said. "There would be no one to sew me up."

The people have always called him simply Dr. G., perhaps because his name is so strange on the tongue. *Carl Gellenthien.* The Spanish people have been coming to him for fifty years, trying to talk to him in a language he has never understood, taking the winding road out of Watrous five miles along the Mora River to Valmora, where the TB sanatorium used to be. Now there was only the clinic, open four days a week. Dr. G. was always there, though, and he never charged much. Five dollars to cure whatever you happened to have.

He closed the door to his library and walked quickly along the dusty corridors of the old hospital. The empty rooms were heavy with relics of bygone medicine—a screened-in sleeping porch, a wicker wheelchair, a metal bed with the mattress folded up, a hot-water bottle, a pneumothorax machine, a bedpan used to store nails and printed diets for tuberculars. In the courtyard, weeds were growing high around rows and rows of abandoned TB cottages; an ancient swing banged against its metal frame, and the face of an old man in a business suit appeared at a darkened window, staring at the doctor passing by in the courtyard.

"Oh, yes. Him," the doctor said without turning. "A TB tramp. He's been to fifteen or twenty hospitals. I guess he likes this one best."

The eighty-five-year-old retired railroad worker was the hospital's last full-time inmate. "Nowhere else to go," the doctor explained. "Not a relative in the world. Why not die here?

He was a patient thirty, forty years ago."

In the great yawn of sun, among the rocks and trees and along the ignoble Mora River winding through the underbrush, time did not matter. Forty years and forty days were the same; they embraced the same constants. The life and death of a wife, a child, a patient, blended into the overall languor, the atrophy that the sanatorium exuded.

In the closet was a skeleton named Lucy, which the state patrol borrowed from time to time and placed in a parked car in order to get motorists to slow down.

Along one wall was a collection of medicine bottles containing things Dr. G. had removed from his patients over the years. They were labeled: "Tick," "Black Widow Spider," "Tapeworm," "Pablo Peña's Right Ear," "Pinworm," "Screw Worm," "Roundworm," "Crab Louse," "Petrified Frijoles" (removed from a woman who said the *bruja* turned them to stone). There was also a large jar labeled: "The heart of a healthy 21 year old truck driver killed in an accident 6.20.64 on the San Francisco Freeway."

The old doctor sat in the chair behind his desk, wearing his white coat and stethoscope even though the patients would not come for an hour yet. He liked this time best, the morning sun streaming in the window, his desk shiny and neat, his books arranged so that he did not have to leave his chair to look things up, the medical souvenirs and the folk medicines in their bottles so he could see them. He was happiest when he was in this office he had known for so long.

"The old days," he sighed, and tried to re-member them. When the horse was the limit of the horizon. When he delivered babies by the light of a kerosene lamp, with the woman lying down on an ironing board, and he went to work with a bottle of Lysol, store string and scissors. The old days. When he was Eisenhower's physician. When he was vice-president of the AMA. When he spent fifteen years in Navajo country curing the Indians of TB. The old days. When a prostitute in Wagon Mound charged fifty cents for her services and he charged a dollar fifty for his. When a patient of his threw her unwanted baby down the privy and he convinced a jury of her innocence. She went on to become a nurse, he said, and a good one too. When Bonney, who hid from the draft for thirty years up the canyon, grabbed a power line and was electrocuted, but came to in the doctor's car, took the cigar out of his mouth and blew smoke rings in his face. The old days. There were so many letters from that time that he had collected them in four huge scrapbooks.

"I need some more pills send me some p.s. I want to go this next week for a shack up."

"Mr. Gellenthien: I am Modesto Pacheco am interestad in medicine. I thought how much you would charge to teach me how to become a medical doctor."

"I'm sending you a picture to show you where my trouble is. The lining of my stomach is not in its proper position. If you could send some medicines for my trouble I would pay the mailman here. P.S. I also have a gallstone but it don't seem to bother much."

"I'm sure worried cause I suppose to come sick the 22nd and I didn't. I'm worried to death that I'm

pregnant. We have always been so careful. But that night the rubber tear up a little."

The letters made Dr. G. laugh. Medicine had changed so much since fifty years ago, when he began. Humanity stepped out when the government stepped in. He said he could not afford malpractice insurance and still keep his rates low enough for the people in Mora County.

"I ought to go to Australia with the rest of them," the doctor grumbled. He stopped and thought about it. "If you want to see a fellow have a real hemorrhage, stick your knife in his pocketbook."

A Spanish man came in and sat down, his face tense. "I got this pain," he said. "I got this pain right here in the liver." He held his side where he believed his liver to be.

"Aurelio," the doctor said, "you live long enough and your liver will be okay."

The general store in Watrous is not so general anymore. A hundred dollars would buy the place out. The shelves are bare and a mustiness hangs in the huge, high-ceilinged building, constructed in the nineteenth century. The place is clean, though, and the cash register polished; but the safe is open and empty. "So they won't rob me," Katie Hand said, watery eyes peering through thick-lensed glasses.

At eighty-five, she knew the value of work, the danger of lying too long in bed. With legs wrapped in thick stockings, a wool hat pulled down over her ears even in summer, with hands deformed by the ravages of arthritis, she still worked ten hours a day, more when the days

A hundred dollars would nearly buy her out, but eighty-five-year-old Katie Hand worries that she stocks too many things. "Maybe I ought to close up. But then what would people do?"

were longer.

"I'm not supposed to work," she announced, small and shriveled behind the counter. "The doctor says slow down. Slow down for what?"

She had given her life to the store, and now that she was alone and nearly forgotten, the store gave her the only life she had. There was importance in arranging six boxes of Quaker

Oats on a shelf built to hold twenty times more; there was social contact to be had with a ranch wife who stopped for a bottle of Clorox; there was always the weather to be discussed and news to be gathered, of children and grandchildren and last year's hired man.

A cat paraded up and down the long counter, sniffing a bin that had one potato in it. The smell of Lysol was strong in the room. It was cold, but she would not turn up the heat. She wore two coats instead.

"Watrous used to be a nice little town," Katie Hand said. "Five hundred people. I used to sell drugs, hardware, shoes, clothes. Used to have two full-time clerks. Customers came from forty miles around. It's Texans that ruined everything. I don't have time for Texans." Her gnarled old hands gripped the counter as if to brace herself against them. She was historian and social commentator, the town's oldest citizen and thus in charge of lamenting its shifting next of kin.

"I don't have time for anything except keeping this place alive."

No one remembers exactly when Katie Hand came from Alabama on the train and opened the store. What people remember is that she held on to every dime she ever made. She was shrewd, the people say. She always knew exactly what you owed and drummed it out of you. The trouble was, nowadays she could not be pleased. If you bought something, she complained that she had to reorder and it took too much time, filling out the slips and all, by looking up the wholesale grocers. If you didn't buy anything, she wondered why she stayed in business.

"People say, I don't know what you see in this place, but I love this little town. Don't know anybody anymore. And half the people that come in would like to rob me. If I went away, that's what they'd do."

To protect her interests, Katie Hand had not been out of Watrous since 1959.

"The year I went to the dentist," she said, seating herself in a folding chair that tilted to one side. One hand clutched the cat to keep it from running away. "He died of a heart attack before he finished me. They tell me I ought to get my teeth fixed. But now I don't have time. Costs five dollars anyway.

"Can't see, either. I had my glasses changed last in '54. Ought to take care of it. But it's money wasted. And besides, I'd have to close the store."

She could not close the store, she said, because of robbers and because of the bus that came through.

"I meet three buses a day, three hundred sixty-five days a year. I've done it eighteen years, summer and winter. I used to meet four, but then they changed the schedule so it gets in late at night. I have to be here or else the driver stops to see if I'm dead. But the one that always stops, they're going to retire him in a year."

There was importance in meeting the bus, even though she didn't sell tickets anymore. There were packages to be left and packages to be sent out; once in a while there was even a passenger getting off. The bus brought the Denver *Post* a day late and news from stops up the line if she was quick enough to be outside when the driver stepped down to catch his breath.

But there was nothing much to tell anymore, not about Watrous or the river or the towns that had lived in her imagination for all those years. If she tried, she might cry over what had been lost and not found again, or found and put away in dread.

"I don't cry," she said, stiffening her pleated upper lip. "I freeze. If you cry you relax, and I can't relax. I can't cry. I hurt in the chest, that's all. It's an awful strain when you can't cry. I held my mother's hand when she died, but I never cried. I'm almost eighty-six years old and I never cried once in my life." She said it with a sense of accomplishment. To be so strong against the world required no more effort than that.

They call the town Watro, leaving off the end deliberately. Who ever heard of a Spanish town called Watrous anyway? It was named that in 1879 after an Anglo, Samuel Watrous, who owned the trading post. Watro. To possess it a little, after all.

In Watro there was once a *bruja,* a witch, and she could make people sick by putting a pin in an old rag doll that was magic. If she wanted you to have a headache, she would stick the pin in the doll's head. If she wanted you to have a stomach ache, she would put the pin there. She could create great sickness with the pin and the rag doll. She had other medicines too. She could put a spell on people and make them die. Not even the doctors could cure such a person.

"That's what happened to my wife," Henry Yara said, standing in front of his little adobe

Henry Yara blames his blindness on the bruja *who also killed his wife.*

house on a back street in Watro. "The *bruja* killed her."

The *bruja* turned herself into an owl and watched Henry's house at night. They could hear her calling, and the more she called, the more sickness there was inside.

Finally Henry Yara's wife died. The owl stopped calling then.

Last summer the *bruja* died too, in her house up the canyon where the *acequia* comes from the

Sheepherder's wagon, in the San Luis valley, is a legacy from pioneer days.

river and irrigates the apple orchard she used to have. Poof. She died just like that. Without being sick at all.

"There is something stronger than a *bruja*," Henry Yara said. "We cannot talk about it too much or else there will be a spell on us. This *bruja* is dead, but there is another *bruja* some-where. She can make us sick even from far away. You cannot hide from her. You can only try and make her stay away."

The *bruja* put a spell on Henry Yara too, long ago when he was thirty years old. Gave him

a sickness and made him blind. He was not ashamed of his blindness. Take a picture of it, he said. To show what the *bruja* did.

In Watro they were not sure that the *bruja* was really dead.

A strange owl had recently come out of the canyon. Sometimes they heard its call at night. Sometimes they thought a big bird was follow-ing them when they walked, but when they turned around, there was nothing there at all.

The *bruja*.

On Fridays, the people of Watro sprinkle

holy water in the corners of their houses to keep the *bruja* out.

The San Luis Valley, as flat and smooth as a tortilla is sixty miles wide. Lying between the Sangre de Cristos and the Continental Divide, the valley is hushed and eerie, and when the wind blows it releases the sound of the ancient sea that used to be there. The wind hollows out the mind, scours the land, which is dry and alkaline, and infuriates the women, who are forever locked in combat with the dust which seeps in and permeates the mattresses as well as the mind. The wind causes the men to plug their ears with cotton soaked in linseed oil whenever they work in the fields. Even then they cannot keep out the moaning of the ancient sea or fully understand what keeps their nerves on edge.

The land is big, but the sky is bigger. It seems to suck at the land, to draw it away from itself, to draw out the energy from the short grass and make it even shorter. Out there, the sky is the great leveler, the supreme ego buster; the

sky is what people remember most when they have traveled somewhere else. The sky is usually a clear electric blue, not yet polluted by the coal plants which have ruined so much of the southwest sky. Here, as the people are fond of saying, there is air that hasn't been breathed before. Here, too, is land not yet "improved" by developers, although along one stretch of road, between Blanca and Alamosa, wind-swept "ranchettes" are blatantly advertised for sale, staked out all across the parched and treeless sage flats. The San Luis valley blooms, thanks to

Top left. *Bean pickers, the San Luis valley.*
Bottom left. *Mr. and Mrs. Victor Lopez have a big vegetable garden and strings of chilis drying in the sun.*
Above left. *The Herminio Mares family lives in a house that has a well in the middle of the kitchen floor.*
Above right. *Luben Vigil, San Antonio.*

a system of artesian wells, for the farmers who raise great crops of potatoes, barley, lettuce, beets and wheat. The rest contend with aridity.

Nearly two thirds of the forty thousand people in the San Luis valley are Spanish and, except for the Utes who were driven out over a century ago, they are the oldest inhabitants of Colorado.

Religious shrine is made of car hood, cross bow and painting of Jesus.

Herminio Mares and his grandchildren. Adobe house has wall-to-wall carpeting inside.

When the Spanish came to the valley around 1850, they moved north from New Mexico, which has always tried to claim this land from Colorado. Even now the San Luis valley seems like a natural extension of New Mexico; there is little difference between the adobe villages of this valley and the ones that lie to the south. The great sweeping land is the same and so are its colors—a blur of muted browns and yellows washed with the dirt red of adobe houses made of mud and straw, with a man's piss mixed in for good luck. They have made no mistake about it. Earth houses are the warmest and the coolest, depending on the time of year; earth houses, being natural, possess the strength of the ground. Earth houses stand from one generation to another, absorbing this man's pain and that man's sorrow; absorbing, too, the children's laughter, the family prayers, the *alabados* sung at Easter, the long-drawn-out cries of women giving birth in narrow rooms. In the backyards, the men have buried their dead infants in shoe boxes or wrapped them in the skin of a goat. There is no money for funerals for those who never lived.

"There'll be another one next year, so I don't feel too bad."

"We didn't give a name to it, seeing it was dead. We just baptized it and gave it back to God."

"We had twelve and raised six and as I said to him, God has a reason for doing that."

"I was a midwife in this valley for forty years. I guess I delivered fifteen hundred babies from Taos to San Luis, in houses that made me sick to walk in. I always had with me a good strong flashlight, some sterile cord and some green soap to wash up with. But I never gave them any germs they didn't have. They were too used to their own."

Like much of New Mexico, the San Luis valley has its superstitions, its folklore, its deeply rooted religion, which is traditional and out of touch with the real needs of its people. One aged Spanish priest in San Luis still calls his parishioners "children," still preaches against birth control and abortion in an area where illegitimacy is higher than the national rate and families average six children or more. One person out of five is on welfare and among those who work, the average income is about seven thousand a year. Alcoholism and suicide rates continue to soar despite state and federal programs aimed at reducing them.

Since 1965, about twelve thousand people—or nearly one fourth of the population—have left the valley in search of city jobs that seldom materialize. But they are also searching for something else, an identity that has managed to elude them despite their family ties and a strong cultural background.

"It's the heritage that's going," said Amadeo Martinez, Costilla County clerk and the fourth generation of his family to live in San Luis. "I remember when a wedding lasted three days. Now it's over in three hours. My father told me when he wanted to marry my mother, he had to ask her father first. Now they don't ask anyone.

Eppemenio Valdez, San Luis, plays a love song on his guitar, which he says has become his woman ever since his wife died.

Main Street, Antonito.

They just do it." In his early forties, Martinez admitted that his own children were missing out on some of their heritage too. "They don't even speak Spanish anymore, except for a few words. We don't talk it in our house the way my parents do. And we don't tell stories about the old days either. The kids would rather watch television."

Turning to his thick record books, Martinez said, "The ones who knew what it was like to be real Spanish, well, they're all in here." He thumped the cover of a musty-smelling book. "Dead."

Amadeo Martinez pushed the book to one side and said, "Those old people were always polite. They were poor but they had this dignity, you know. It was like they were saying: Take my sheep and my goats and my house. But not this in here." He pointed to the heart. "They had their own kind of humor too. I remember one time when my father-in-law, Maclovio Gallegos, was going down the street and some tourists stopped him and said, 'How high are you here?' He didn't stop walking. He just looked up at the sky and told them, 'Oh, pretty close to heaven.' "

Martinez laughed good-naturedly, then leaned forward. "There are a few of them still around. Maclovio is still alive. So is Eppe Valdez. The ones who would be called *don*, if this were a different time."

Don Eppemenio Valdez was eighty-eight years old and he was living in a pink trailer house on a side street in San Luis, next door to his daughter. For sixty years he had been a *sovador*, a chiropractor, and he could still work on the body and make it feel good, he said, were it not for the fact that his eyes were giving out.

"I was going to become a doctor," he said in Spanish, for he spoke no English, "but I thought: No one will come to me. My people have never trusted these doctors. So I went up to Alamosa to Dr. Stevens and for two hundred dollars he taught me all I know."

He had been a Penitente for half a century too, a member of the Sociedad de Nuestro Padre Jesús de Nazareno, which had been in San Luis for as long as he could remember. "When I first went in, there were seventy members, but now I have buried almost everyone. No, we don't meet anymore. What is the use? No one is left." He was sad for a moment, then his face exploded into a grin. "I don't want to be thinking about all my friends who have gone away. I

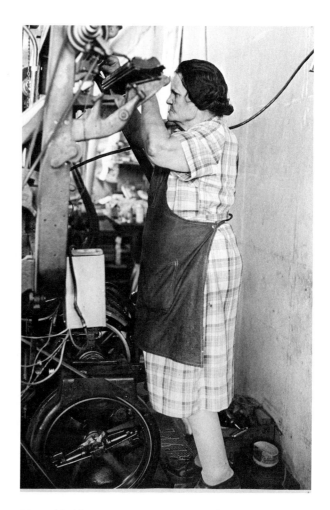

Mary Mudd, seventy-nine-year-old publisher of the La Jara Gazette. *"This machine's older than I am. We've got a new one, but it doesn't make the kind of noise I'm used to."*

want to sing a song to keep myself busy."

He got out his guitar and began to sing all the old Spanish songs that his mother had taught him, in a voice that was still clear and passionate.

"Now," said Don Eppemenio, "I will sing you a love song that I learned many years ago."

He shut his eyes and put his head back and caressed the strings, gently, so that only the

softest sounds came out and joined his voice, which was filled with tenderness and joy.

When at last he was through, Don Eppemenio bent his head over his instrument and let his fingers rest on the frets. "My wife died in 1961," he said. "Ever since then my guitar has been my woman and my whiskey." He lifted his head and laughed and began to play a new song, using some words of his own:

"Someday I'll die but you will remember me, my love. You will remember my song."

The bar in Antonito was like any other in the West. A Coors beer sign glowed above the rows of liquor bottles; a Falstaff sign blazed above the freshly washed glasses. In the middle of the room two men were playing pool beneath a lighted shade that advertised Budweiser. But there was something different. A hand-lettered sign near the cash register advised: "No Feets of Strength at the Bar." Near it, another one warned: "No Hats on the Dance Floor."

The bartender's name was Cletus, he said, and he worked there only part time, being a carpenter by trade. "I'm twenty-two years old," he said, drawing a glass of beer for himself and skimming off the foam with his finger. "I've lived in Antonito all my life. People tell me there's no future here, but what I say is, there's no future anyplace else. I left here once when I was eighteen and went to L.A. I could have made a lot of money and maybe had this future that everyone says is out there. But what I saw was just a way to make a living, so I came home. What I think is, a little place like Antonito has all the peace I'm ever going to need."

HAVE A NICE DAY, FROM THE BEE GEE'S GANG

Opposite top. *David Cook, alias Lone Wolf, and Marilyn Garrett, Mineral Hot Springs. "We tried to open a cafe, but some ranchers came in one night and wrecked it."*
Opposite bottom. *Tony Lucero, owner of the Palace Hotel, Antonito. "I've had this hotel for forty years and the only thing I've changed are the sheets."*
Above. *Bee Gee's Café, Alamosa.*

Antonio Lucero stood in the middle of his alfalfa field east of Antonito, watching the big new air-conditioned Hesston swather being driven by his fifteen-year-old grandson, Serafin, the fifth generation of Luceros to work the land.

"Last year we put up sixty thousand bales,"

Augustine Villareal, a railroad worker for fifty-five years, lives with his wife in Juanita, along the San Juan River. "She calls me a hippie, so I guess I'll have to go on welfare and learn how to smoke the marijuana."

he said. "This year it will be even more."

Antonio Lucero was seventy-six and looked twenty years younger. His face, which was the color of a saddle, had etched into it the pride of continuity and of land, the self-assurance that comes when a man has lived all his life in one place and thus earns the right to claim it for his own. In that part of the West, five generations was forever; five generations had produced roots so deep that now, to one watching a strong man gather up the yield of a strong land, it was hard to tell if the man had bettered the land or the land had bettered the man.

Old men of the land are prone to the recitation of historical facts which separate them from the newcomers, who arrived on the soil only a half century or so ago. If a man has been in a place long enough, he becomes convinced not only of his entitlement to the land but to the privilege that goes with it. His word becomes

Margarita Lucero greets an old friend in San Rafael, a village not far from where her family settled in 1850.

the last on everything; his name lends credibility to causes and greases the political machine; his net worth guarantees position on rural bank, school and church boards. What is due such a man is not only respect for his familial influence, but wordless recognition for the legacy he has carried on. In a country so new, there are few traditions. Inherited land is one of them.

"My grandfather was Antonio Domingo Lucero and he came here in 1856 from Albuquer-

que," Tony Lucero said. "That was twenty years before Colorado became a state. He homesteaded south of Manassa on 160 acres, mostly corn and wheat. He wasn't here long before he drowned trying to cross the Rio Grande. Then it was up to his children, including my father, who was born in 1859 in a cabin way over there." He pointed east, across the shimmering alfalfa field, soft and sweet-smelling in the morning heat.

"My father, Aniceto Lucero, homesteaded with his brother at the head of Fox Creek in

1912. Some of the land he bought for $1.50 an acre back when all people thought about was growing things on it and not holding on to it for real estate profit. They proved up on 640 acres each and when he died, he left me this land and then I bought what my uncle had. At one time my family had 8,500 head of sheep and what that meant was enough wool and mutton to supply nearly half the state—but of course they were all eating beef at the time."

Margarita Lucero came out, as always, to see what her husband was doing and to watch how well Serafin maneuvered the big Hesston, sitting high in its luxurious cab. If Antonio's roots went back far, hers went even farther.

"My grandfather settled here in 1850," she said, "but some people say it was not until 1852. If you want, I'll show you where he was."

It was important to know about such things, for it was what heritage meant; it was important to understand the consistency of so many generations willing to kill themselves for the sake of mastering the land. Was it challenge or foolhardiness? Livelihood or lack of choice? Passing the graveyard where her ancestors were buried, Margarita Lucero remarked, "I don't believe there was another life they would have had."

As these people once prayed to the Virgin Mary during the droughts, the diseases which wiped out children and the disasters which finally broke the men, they might have asked if there was another life they were *meant* to have. Somehow, the land still reflects the pain of those generations; their sweat has been turned over many times with the soil; their tears swallowed up by thirsty fields. The land aches, resists and finally yields because the generations were patient, expecting neither too much nor too little from it.

Margarita Lucero sat on the steps of the solid adobe house that her father had built in 1922, lived in now by a sister and a nephew who kept his motorcycle on the porch. The house was home and the land was home. She pointed out the fields that her grandfather had plowed and the hill where he always rode to watch for Indians. And there, crumbling in the sun, were the remains of the adobe house where she had been born in 1908, one of eighteen children.

"I was quarantined here for forty days with scarlet fever," she said, standing in front of bricks that were only knee-high now. Intact were only the thick beams that her father had cut in the mountains far to the west; even now she could see the notches his ax had made.

There was so much memory and so much living there on her grandfather's homestead that finally Margarita Lucero said, "My father taught me that the land will always give you back whatever you put into it. Sometimes I think that what he meant was it would never leave you. I have seen some tragedy in my life and when it happens, it is always this place that I come to." Her fine, dark eyes went out over the family fields. Only a summer or two before, her little grandson had been crushed beneath a tractor there.

"I don't know what it is," she murmured. "This land . . ." She did not finish, nor did she have to. The land was written all across her face.

Top right. *Frank and Chris Chavez, ranchers, San Juan River valley. "When Mom got sick I said to Chris, I'll cook if you learn how to fix her hair."*

Bottom right. *Ophelia and Felix Gomez in front of the general store he ran for fifty-five years in Pagosa Junction, population now three.*

The town is not a town anymore; it is a ghost lying in a bend along the San Juan River, where the cottonwoods grow thick and the sage-covered hills roll away from the valley, higher and higher, so that the town seems protected and even lost among them. Pagosa Junction is not on the map and to get there requires a thirty-mile journey from Pagosa Springs over a winding washboard road that passes through what is left of Lone Tree and connects half a dozen ranches along the way.

Pagosa Junction used to have a hundred people living in it, but now there were only three— Juan Jose Peña, a Pueblo Indian, and Felix and Ophelia Gomez, who could trace their Spanish lineage back to the eighteenth century. The Gomezes had lived there long enough to know that the world was bounded by the river to the south and to the north by the white church on top of the hill, to which the same priest had been coming since 1932. It was in this church that they had been married on February 12, 1923, a year after Ophelia had come up from New Mexico to play the organ on St. John the Baptist Day.

The train hasn't run through Pagosa Junction since 1968, the same year that Felix Gomez closed the dry goods store he had operated there since 1913. But the habit of waiting for the train was hard to break, so at precisely eleven-fifteen one morning he took out his 1916 railroad watch and looked at it, the way he always did. He stopped what he was saying to listen for the long-gone sound of the steam engine pulling around the last bend in the river before it chugged to a halt outside his door to take on water from the tank, its water spout, like some headless chicken, dripping onto the tracks.

Felix Gomex got up from the chair and went to the door of his new trailer house and looked out at the old building across the way, which used to be his store. Perhaps he did not really see the faded red storefront with its wooden veranda in need of repair or the rusted Conoco pump tilting crazily into the wind or the grass growing between the rails of the little bit of railroad track that was left. Old eyes, like old memories, tend to focus on the past. Felix Gomez, the *don* of the San Juan River valley, the gentleman shopkeeper of simpler times, knew what was happening.

"I had a cataract operation this summer," he said. "They told me I'd see better. But what do I want to see better for? I've seen enough already."

It was eleven thirty and time for the train to go and for Don Felix to mount his horse and check his flock of sheep, which had drifted down close to the river.

"Every day I ride my horse," he said. "We are growing old together." There was laughter behind his face. "But that horse complains much more than I do."

Ophelia Gomez waited until her husband went out, then she put water on for coffee and spoke about what was most heavily on her mind.

"All my bones were dissolved with this ar-

At eighty-four, Felix Gomez still tends his sheep and rides his horse every day.

thritis," she said solemnly. "They're very soft and there is pain all the time. I don't bother Felix with it. What's the use of two people suffering? I kiss my pain and say, It's not going to hurt." She raised her twisted fingers to her lips. "My little pets. I have to humor this hand. I have to tell it to be strong. Every day, as old as I am, I make myself a little better. I read and discuss so many books—right now I am reading about Archbishop Lamy of Santa Fe. And I

travel too—all over the world with the *Geographics*."

She did not have to go anywhere to know what the world was about, for the world came to her door every day to see what the store contained. In Pagosa Junction, nostalgia had become a commodity, not to be sold but to be given away, in the store that was like a museum, with everything exactly as Don Felix had left it ten years before.

"You can see what you want to see here," Don Felix said later, opening the shades to let the sunshine in. "Up there are some old Indian baskets that the Apaches used to pay me with. They lived just over the hill toward Dulce, and they'd come in once a month on horseback with these baskets. They weren't worth ten dollars then."

Behind the baskets was a row of calendars, beginning with 1919 and going until 1954. There were flatirons, coffee mills, a tobacco cutter, a slot machine, some religious paintings— and a picture of FDR.

"Here are real silk stockings," Doña Ophelia said, and held them up. "Here are buttons made of glass." In the store, she knew what people wanted to see.

"Look at my bear," Don Felix said, pointing to the skin and head draped across the only place to sit down. "I shot him in 1912. He's still as good as new."

"I lived in this store for fifty-three years," Doña Ophelia said, opening the door behind the office, where her husband was going through mail that was ten years old. There was a living room with tinted pictures of her family

Felix Gomez and Juan Jose Peña. "I have known him seventy years. He calls me primo *and I call him* primo.*"*

still on the wall. "That's my mother after she had twelve children. She was still small, still beautiful, and that was why my father loved her. You can tell it from his smile. We have a deep background, Felix and I. We have always used the common sense our parents gave us. We have had a beautiful life. We've looked at it straight. We never fought; we always sat down and figured it out. But there's not too much to understand anymore, because we know each other too well."

She closed the door on her memories and turned to find Don Felix still sorting through his mail. "Here is a three-cent stamp," he said. "Here is a postcard from Germany after the war." But his wife was at the front of the store, opening a drawer.

"Look at this beautiful beaded shawl," Doña Ophelia said. "I wore it to a dance one time. See how finely it is made, the work, the love that

went into it. Nothing is made that way anymore." She wrapped it around her shoulders, over her cotton blouse, and found a mirror behind a life-size cutout of Santa Claus and an ancient post office sign.

"Come," said Don Felix, drawing the shades so the hot sun would not ruin anything. "We will go see Peña."

He picked up his walking stick and went down the dusty road to the one-room house where the Indian lived. "He's ninety-four years old," Felix Gomez said, "and I am eighty-four. We've known each other seventy years. I call him *primo* and he calls me *primo.* Peña, I say to him, that is a very long time."

Juan Jose Peña came out and sat down on a bench, turning his face to the sun. He spoke to Don Felix in Spanish about the season that was turning and about the sheep Don Felix had. Soon he would go away for the winter, south where it was warm. When spring came, he would come back to Pagosa Junction, where he had his home and his friend.

Suddenly Juan Jose Peña got up and went inside, and he came out with a picture of himself, taken when he was six or seven years old, with Red Ryder, who was touring in a Wild West show. He looked at the picture and ran his fingers over the glass, then went inside again and came out wearing his war bonnet.

"Take a picture," old Peña said. "I used to be a war chief once."

With his war bonnet falling over his shoulders, Juan Jose Peña went out into the dirt yard to pick out a spot where he could see down to the river and past it to the hills where he and Don Felix used to ride, the Indian teaching the white man how to hunt for game. He saw, as Don Felix so often saw, that what was past was not really gone at all, that he had kept it alive merely by living where he was as long as he had.

Later that day, Doña Ophelia fixed supper in the trailer, then played "Somewhere Over the Rainbow" on the little organ that was set up in the living room, her twisted fingers dragging the music out of the keys. When she was finished, she and Don Felix moved to their little porch to watch the sun go down, remarking that the evenings were beginning to turn cool now that fall was coming on.

"We talk about death, Felix and I," Doña Ophelia said. "When it comes time, we want to be buried up there on the hill. We've already picked out a tree. One little juniper will be enough—why use two? No stone, no marker of any kind. We want to lie there and look out at everything we've ever known." Her face was sweet and gentle, and if she was used to anything, it was the peacefulness of their forgotten little town.

"In a few years, you must wander up in those hills and see where we are," Don Felix said, mostly to himself.

Before the fall was out, he was gone, quickly and quietly in his sleep. He had ridden his horse on the day he died, helping a neighbor to round up stray cattle in the canyon not far from home. The people of the valley buried him exactly where he wanted to be. But they put up a marker by the juniper tree.

MOUNTAINS

From a distance, Cripple Creek looks like a toy town under a Christmas tree. The streets are symmetrical and push toward the horizon; the church steeple punctuates the thin, high air; the brick courthouse is in its correct position of authority and reprimand; even the train station is carefully placed to make the most of the view. Far to the west, a chain of snow-capped mountains is pasted against a cloud-smudged sky that is the same shade of blue as the land; looking from a windswept hillside a hundred miles away, it is hard to tell which is which. Earth and sky the same.

The wind always blows from these mountains, straight across the rangeland into the wilderness, down into the bowl where Cripple Creek is spread out, and up again to the chunky, ignoble backside of Pikes Peak, which always repels the wind from the west. Hump-backed hills ring the little town of Cripple Creek. Up and away they rise, covered with a unique pattern of burro trails and surface mines which stand out like skin eruptions—the dried-up sores of nearly a century ago, when twenty thousand men answered the cry "Gold!"

They came up the pass from Colorado Springs, on horses and burros, and later by stagecoach and train, to Colorado's last big gold strike, a frenzy of hard rock stiffs and European syndicators, of unknown men who struck it rich and rich men who struck it even richer. It was a time for luck and risk and just plain hope. Thousands threw up tents and staked their claims, most to die in debt and obscurity, others to sell their holdings for just enough money to get to the next mountain range. It was the illusion of wealth that drove them on, the reckless gamble that was more important than the discovery of gold itself.

Cripple Creek and Victor, nine miles south, wear their history like a moth-eaten cloak. They drag it out of the closet in summer, when tourists take the winding road from Colorado Springs and, cameras in hand, seek to find an antidote for routine lives. If the gold era represented a wisp of pioneer discovery, the tourists want it on film, to take back home as verification of the high truth to be found in a jumble of ore dumps, decaying boardinghouses, mill offices, miners' shacks, cheap hotels and starkly outlined gallows frames. In their pictures of nostalgic junk is the suggestion of what the guidebooks say gold mining had to be—a tough and glamorous adventure, never mind corruption, thievery, lung disease, cholera, water in the mines and bloody labor disputes. Never mind the true-life adventures in the cemetery either—babies who died before their first birthday; mothers who died in childbirth ("I'll meet you in heaven," one tombstone says); miners who all died on the same day when a shaft caved in; the good men and women for whom hard work was merely a synonym for dying before their time.

In the 1890s, this twenty-four-square-mile District, as it is known, had five hundred mines, which over a seventy-year period paid out twenty million ounces of gold ore worth eight hundred million dollars, more than the California and Alaska strikes combined. There were twenty-five houses of prostitution along

Above. *Cripple Creek looks like a toy town lying in a bowl west of Pikes Peak.*
Overleaf. *Goldfield, windswept and nearly deserted, faces tip of Pikes Peak, elevation 14,110 feet.*

Myers Avenue, fifty-four trains a day into Victor, roulette wheels, opium dens, claim jumpers, train robbers, three-dollar-a-day miners and one hundred fifty saloons. Mr. Gallagher and Mr. Sheen were trainmen in Victor; Texas Guinan sang her love songs there; Lowell Thomas was born in a little house on the side of a hill; and Jack Dempsey trained for the heavy-weight championship of the world not far from the ore dumps that rise three hundred feet above the town.

History is often spelled *f-a-n-t-a-s-y* and facts are often nothing more than bait to lure the bored and unsuspecting. In Cripple Creek and Victor, it is not only the glory of yesterday which is stirring men's minds again but the fantasy-fact that in a certain geological quirk—a four-by-six-mile basin of hard rock ore—there is the mother lode just waiting to be dug out, an undiscovered fortune reputed to be worth at least ten billion dollars. A thousand miles of tunnels—dark, silent and more often filled with water than not—beckon to big-time speculators and two-bit operators alike. This time the price is right. Now that gold has risen to $180 an ounce and more, there is a profit to be made, if anyone can figure out how to mine gold for less money than it brings on the open market.

The new gold rush, if it comes, will be backed by such sophisticated money as the Golden Cycle Corporation, itself backed by the oil money of Texas Gulf. Golden Cycle has been around Cripple Creek since the last century, owns sixty percent of the land in the District and all the mineral rights under the town of Victor. The Stratton estate, heirs to the childless Winfield Scott Strattons' fifteen million-dollar fortune, has title to about thirty percent of the land, with a few small mining companies and individual speculators owning the rest.

George Schrank came up from the three-hundred-foot level of the Mary Nevin mine and stepped out of the skip carrying an ore sample in a plastic sandwich bag. He looked around the

John Nothaus, left, and his father, Albert, right, are both gold miners, live in Goldfield, population thirty. "Gold mining just gets in your blood. I wouldn't want to do a whole lot else."

desolate, snow-covered mine site to make sure no one was watching. After years of backbreaking work, he was now within three weeks of bringing the first ore out. In the hoist house, a big sign promised: MARCH 1. Among Schrank and his nine employees there was an air of excitement, a hint of the kind of strike that in the old days had made millionaires out of ordinary men. George Schrank tucked his ore sample in his pocket and tried to contain himself.

"I had the Mary Nevin until this year," the miner said, standing beside the recently constructed gallows frame, painted a blazing orange. "I worked five years and sank $125,000 into her and still we weren't mining gold. I went public a couple of months ago. We raised $500,000 in three days. That's what gold speculation is all about." He smiled to reveal a mouthful of gold-capped teeth; his gold-

rimmed spectacles reflected the old mine dump; and when he spoke the word "gold," it came out reverent and honeyed.

"But now we've gone public, we can't say anything about gold," George Schrank said, scanning the ground and the timbers that would be used to stabilize the shaft. "We can say we've gained access to the inner working of the mine. We can say we've begun a limited exploration and sampling program. We can say we've retimbered the shaft down to three hundred feet and installed a high-pressure air line. We can say we've improved the mill so it meets state, federal and company safety standards. And that's about all we can say."

George Schrank, whose truck once bore a bumper sticker that advised "Keep It Small, Keep It All," had obviously changed his outlook. He trudged over the frozen ground to the

Paul Shook, left, geologist for the Mary Nevin mine, receives an ore sample from George Schrank in the old mill house, refurbished to process the Mary Nevin's gold production.

assay office with his ore sample. After speaking briefly to Paul Shook, a geologist who sat in the neon-lighted mill laboratory surrounded by shelves of chemicals, machines and scales, he noted that the assay would be completed by a method of atomic absorption.

Then he came back out into the cold, dry air and waited for two young miners, Ted Johnson and Ed Heida, who were new to the District, to come up in the skip. He was anxious to see what they had found while he had been on top.

"The Mary Nevin," George Schrank said fondly, as if she were a lover. "She produced a million in gold and she's only down four hundred feet. That's nothing. The way I figure it, there's 120,000 ounces of gold left in her. At today's prices, that's worth right around twelve million dollars; more if the price goes up."

For Schrank, now past sixty, it was the

dream of a lifetime spent mostly in Milwaukee as a steel inspector for a company manufacturing automobile frames. For others the dream of gold is neither promising nor profitable. The dreamers come and go, stymied by the lack of capital necessary to retimber the old mines, not to mention what it will take to dig out the gold, some of it four thousand feet below the ground. After five years of effort to reach the thousand-foot level of the Ruby mine, Jack Hull went back to Oklahoma, insisting, "We all have big plans. We're all going to make it one way or the other." And Dale Weaver, with twenty-five partners and $200,000 in starting money, shut down his El Paso mine after a disastrous fire destroyed not only the gallows frame but about four hundred feet of the shaft as well.

The old miners, who have lived all their lives among the ruins of the last gold strike, watch

George Schrank owned the Mary Nevin mine for five years before he went public. "The way I figure it, there's 120,000 ounces of gold left in her."

Ted Johnson, left, and Ed Heida, right, after a day in the Mary Nevin mine. The miner's candle is used to detect the presence of gas.

the newcomers ironically, scornful of new methods, such as leaching, and new miners, who all seem to have long hair. In snug Victorian houses, paid for by a lifetime working underground in conditions that often produced silicosis, the old miners remember what they want to remember and hide their high grade—ore stolen from the mines—under their beds, insurance against the uncertainty of the times.

"I'm the only one left on the Cresson," said Jimmy Sterrett, at eighty-four the oldest man born in Cripple Creek who was still living there. It was a distinction that brought people to his door, wanting to know what secrets he had about such a life, getting instead relentless history and well-used miner's jargon. A *drift*, he would say, is a horizontal digging which gets its name because "you just find the vein and drift

Swedish-born Axel Olson, eighty-four, was a Victor miner for fifty years. "The mines were never glamorous the way they tell you. To me it was just life."

miner's status comes not only from the peril and incomprehensibility of the job but from the satisfaction that it happened long ago, back there.

"What do old miners do?" Axel Olson asked, his gentle face encircled by the smoke from his pipe. "They play cards and kill time. Some of them drink and tell stories. The mines were never glamorous the way they tell you. To me it was just a life."

Articulate far beyond his eighth-grade education, Axel Olson at eighty-four had a transcendent beauty and a serenity that had nothing to do with sixty years as a miner. He left Sweden shortly before his twenty-first birthday because he did not want to serve in the army ("I am not a violent man"). He never went back. He married, came to Victor, raised seven children, and spent most of his life working at the Ajax mine, just up the hill from his house. His wife was dead now, his children gone. Out of habit, he always looked out the windows at his past— at the old ore dump from the Ajax, with miners' homes built right on it, and ore houses and gallows frames perched on top, eerie now in their abandonment. His history was in the 360-degree view of the mines he had worked and the houses he had lived in and the streets he walked even now; Axel Olson's history was there at 9,600 feet, amid memory and a nagging doubt that he had done the right thing with his life. ("If I had it to do over, I would not have been a miner. I would have become an educated man.") Circumstance and fate had cast him in an alien role in an alien land, but Axel Olson had learned to make the best of things.

"You only earned four-fifty a day," he said,

along with it." A *stope* is a large vertical excavation that goes up from a tunnel; a *winze* is a shaft that goes down from a tunnel. A stope is laced with *stulls,* or timbers, over which the miners dragged their machines as they worked upward, sometimes to the surface of the mine itself.

They don't expect anyone to understand their lingo and that is part of the plan; an old

Ore dump from the Ajax Mine looms above Victor.

"so at Christmas they made it up to you. When ore was worth ninety-four dollars a ton, we got a five-dollar gold piece. When the ore petered out, we got two cigars. Then we didn't get anything."

He rocked in his chair the way old men do, keeping a rhythm with a past that had its own beat, its own insistence. "When I leave Victor, I'm not going to town," he announced. "I'm going to heaven and look around."

In the presence of Axel Olson, one had the feeling that heaven would be the better for him.

Down the hill from Axel's house, another old miner sat in his living room and gave his thoughts on the subject.

"You know what a gold mine is?" Loren Robb asked, his bushy eyebrows knitted together, his fingers hooked in the straps of his bib overalls. "A hole in the ground owned by a bunch of liars." He had lived in Victor all his sixty-two years and had worked seventeen years in the mines. "All that you needed to be a miner was a forty-four jumper suit and a number two hat. Books never made a miner out of any man. I worked in the Sitting Bull and the Clyde and the Ajax, the Vindicator and the King Solomon, and it didn't do anything for me. I near went crazy underground."

It was not the mines that were important to him, but the fact that he was a survivor of Pearl Harbor, a veteran and a patriot.

"I fought the Japs for forty months in the Pacific," he said, "and I came back with a hundred-percent disability. As a veteran I can tell you I've read the Declaration of Independence, the Constitution, the Bill of Rights and the Bible. Nowhere does it say that you women are equal to us men."

He was a man used to getting a quick response; and getting none, he continued.

Pearl Harbor veteran Loren Robb, Victor, remembers his forty months in the navy. "The flag was what us boys was glad to die for. Now patriotism is a dirty word except to us World War veterans."

"I've had three wives and ten children that I know of. Every time I kick one of these Victor kids in the pants, though, I wonder."

Around Victor, Loren Robb was known as a radical even more right-wing than the town's ultraconservative population. People tended to dismiss his views as the rantings of an eccentric, yet because of his apparent knowledge of everything from legal procedure to psychology, he had become an authority on government, called upon to settle local squabbles over minor points of law.

A prodigious writer of letters to the editors of newspapers around the state, Robb pounded home his theme of patriotism, winding it around his major issue—down with equal rights for women—to prove, however illogically, his point that veterans deserved to be heard. He also wrote frequent letters of complaint to the Victor city hall, signing them: "A genuine man, a genuine Christian, and a 100% disabled veteran." His envelopes were always stamped: "Equal Rights is the Song of the Communists."

His tirade against women finished, Loren Robb got up and looked out the window at the remains of a mine on a distant hill. "If we ever found that rich store of ore over on the Cresson, we'd be in business," he said, mostly to himself. "They've got that big conventional drift right through her. All we'd have to do is run a fast electric train through the Ajax to get to it. It's gassy, though. A damn left-handed Irishman like me is the only one that can work back there. But I'm all broke down in the back and legs."

For a moment there was in his eyes the naked look of a man who had experienced too much pain. Then it passed and he was in his role again, his head turned to a war poster.

"You don't want to crowd us Pearl Harbor boys too much. We might get excited again."

The town of Victor is eerie in its semiconsciousness. Most of the buildings along its

The Victor Elks Club displays its World War II honor roll on either side of the door.

bumpy streets are falling down; in the windows, tattered lace curtains, brass beds and china dolls wait out a strange reprieve from demolition or decay. It is as though there were expectation instead of silence, promise instead of inevitable demise. Victor has managed to coexist with its glorified past, comfortable with the ruins that surround it.

On the sides of the old buildings, faded signs still offer fifty-cent rooms, five-cent cigars, courteous undertaking and whiskey for medicinal purposes. Opposite the Elks Club, with its honor roll of World War II veterans displayed on either side of the door, is a Bob and Wave Salon, with a 1942 calendar in the window. Along the main street, a weird window display features two moth-eaten deer dressed in white jackets, bandages and earmuffs, one in a wheelchair, the other lying in bed. One deer holds an empty whiskey bottle in its lap; on the wall a cryptic

message reads: "Last Survivors of the First Run to Victor from the North Pole December 24, 1891."

Next door to the hospitalized deer, Dr. A. C. Denman, who has been the only doctor in the District for fifty years, has his office; now, however, he sees patients only one hour a day. Opposite the doctor's office, the drugstore window has an unusual display of a cystoscope, a fountain syringe, an ancient x-ray machine and jars of mysterious compounds labeled "Bone Set," "Prickly Ash Bark" and "Skunk Cabbage Root." There are ore buckets on the corner and burros roaming the streets. There is also a certain malaise among the old miners, many of whom hang out at the two local bars, watching strangers come in and go out, rolling dice for the price of a drink and talking with their friends about the way life used to be.

For half a century Lillian Clark has been serving drinks at the Gold Coin Bar, listening to

Victor Mayor Bill Murphy, left, and Richard Myers, right. "Would you believe this guy's our mayor? Most of the business in this town gets done right here in the bar."

the miners' tales, good-naturedly accepting their complaints, chiding them about their lack of wisdom and their debts. At eighty-two, she still works twelve hours a day every day except Tuesday, when she closes and takes a little rest. The bar is her world, the customers her surrogate family, because her only son and her grandchildren are far away in Detroit.

"Oh, I come in and sweep the floors for her," said Richard Myers, perched on a bar stool, a twinkle in his eye. "I look out for her, you know. But then, she looks out for me." He had even got her a Christmas tree, but she refused to turn on the lights.

"Didn't want to waste the electricity," Richard said, watching Lil turn off all the overhead lights now that the sun was coming through the windows. "That Lillian. She could buy Victor, give it back, and still have enough to get by on."

Despite the generation or more that separated them, it was obvious that Lillian Clark was someone special in Richard Myers' life.

He was going on fifty-four, he said, and he had been separated from his wife a long time; he had three children, one of whom worked as a hoist man for the Mary Nevin. "You'd think the kid would have more sense than to get mixed up in a life like this," Richard said, but clearly it was the only life he knew.

"I done everything in the mines," he said, draining the last of his whiskey and ordering another under Lillian's watchful eye. "I run a stoper, a Lyner drill, the cross bar, a muck machine, a square point and the jack legs." Now, with all the old mines closed and the new ones hiring only younger men, Richard Myers was unemployed.

"It was a good life, though," he said. "I

At the city hall, Mayor Bill Murphy visits with City Clerk Betty Groves. Sign above door reads: "Every tyrant comes into power under the pretense of being a protector. Thomas Jefferson."

loved it underground. No two days was alike. The temperature was always the same, summer and winter, and there was always some new ore to sink your pick into. When I came up and saw snow on the ground and so many problems to face, I just felt like pulling on the old cord and going back down." If a man was a true miner, he just naturally liked it better underground, Richard Myers said.

Bill Murphy, the mayor of Victor, came in then, a burly, somber man dressed in a navy-blue jumpsuit, white socks and bedroom slippers. He ordered a drink and glanced over his shoulder to see who was there. Except for Richard Myers, everyone in the bar ignored him. This was because he was an outsider, having lived in Victor only six years; he had come up from Colorado Springs, where he had been a plumber for thirty years.

"Now I'm a plumber here," Bill Murphy said, "and I don't make near as much as I used to. Seven-fifty a service call. But I own the laundry down the block and the pastry parlor too. A lot of people don't like me, but I got them a new water system. That was my platform, a million-dollar deal." He said it as if he expected gratitude, but in Victor there was none.

Murphy's election (135 people voted) and the water system to replace one that was eighty years old have met with mixed feelings in Victor, now obligated for a forty-year, five-percent bond that cost $350,000, the rest being met through federal grants. Some residents say they did not need the water system despite the fact that the old one kept blowing out, that it costs too much money ($750) to hook up to it and that the town, mostly filled with pensioners, cannot even afford the bond.

Above. *Sharon Chenoweth and Victor patrolman Manuel Dixon are the only audience at city council meeting. Question: "Why does your flag have only forty-eight stars? Answer: "What do we care about Alaska and Hawaii? We'll never go there."*

James Keeler, left, and Philip Ussery, right, Victor city council members, ponder problems of new water system at a town meeting.

After a while Bill Murphy got up and went down the block to the silver-painted city hall, built in 1900. Above the door was a sign placed by Loren Robb: "Every tyrant comes into power under the pretense of being a protector. Thomas Jefferson."

Betty Groves, the city clerk, was there attending to her books. A mother of seven who ran for office "because it's hard to get by on one pay check," she had been at her job less than six months. One of her duties was to read Loren Robb's letters at the city council meetings twice a month.

"That way he gets to be heard," she said, "but then, you never know when he's going to

Judge Margaret Tekavee of Cripple Creek. "I've known these people all my life, but when they come in here it's as though we never met." Calendar is for a blank book and lithography firm.

come down and give us a speech. I asked him one day, What's the difference between communism and socialism and democracy? He said, You've got to watch those isms."

She laughed and went to the wall safe and produced her favorite piece of Victor memorabilia. It was a yellowed, much-folded receipt dated July 12, 1929. It read: "Received of Wm. Lehr, chief of police Victor 5 gal kegs of moonshine whisky containing about 20 gals and empty bottles, 4 pint bottles full. JG Chillson, Sheriff, Teller County."

Behind Betty Groves' office was the police station, paneled in plastic wood. A big stove protruded toward the middle of the room. Along one wall was Jack Dempsey's signature, scrawled there in 1926; for fifty years the town had painted around it.

The new police chief sat at his desk and dis-

cussed the problems that Victor, population 259, was facing those days.

"We're not Starsky and Hutch up here," Police Chief Eddie Roy said, referring to keeping his eye on things. "Last year we had twenty arrests, but they were mostly hippies. Our local people obey the law. The trouble is all with the hippies. They come up here with drugs, barbiturates mostly. Last year we busted one and thought it was a big crime, but when it got to court in Colorado Springs, they threw it out."

The dungeonlike Victor jail had not been used in thirty years, so when Chief Roy needed to lock people up, they were carted off to the Cripple Creek jail, only slightly more modern than the one in Victor. The year before, he had locked up only ten people who then appeared before the county judge, Margaret Tekavee. She had been in office since 1955, and people said

Victor Police Chief Eddie Roy at his desk in the city hall. On the wall behind him is Jack Dempsey's signature, scrawled there in 1926. The wall has been painted around it.

she was fair, even if she was a woman and even if she hadn't been born there but came to town when she was five years old. Margaret Tekavee was not a lawyer, but she had taken correspondence courses on the subject and everybody agreed that was good enough.

"People come up here and think they're going to get away with something," Eddie Roy said, sitting stiffly in his chair. "Our boys let them know we're around. Once an hour they check the town, just to see who's here. If a car's parked in one spot more than five or six hours we'll check to see if it's stolen." Usually it's not, but the Victor police force is there anyway, keeping surveillance from their cruisers.

In Victor, the word "hippie" is anathema. Not long ago, a house that had half a dozen hippies in it was attacked in the middle of the night. Guns were fired through the window,

but the young people were asleep on the floor. They got out of town the next day.

"I spent a week cutting six loads of cordwood," said a patron at Lil Clark's bar. "It got stole by hippies. Now I got two guns in the pickup and a case of ammunition at home."

And Ohrt Yeager, a former miner, now the owner of Zeke's Place, a block down from Lil's, when asked what he would do if hippies tried to take over the town, replied evenly, "There's a lot of mine shafts around."

But Richard Myers, pointing out the house where the hippies had been shot at, said, "Aw, people up here talk a lot. It's a nice, friendly little town. I'm gonna spend the rest of my life right here."

Two days later he was dead, having frozen to death on the porch of his home, while trying to unlock the door in an inebriated state. He had spent that final Saturday night in Lillian's Gold Coin Bar drinking with his friends.

Two hundred miles southwest of Victor is the little town of Hesperus, marked with a sign that says: "Entering Louis L'Amour Country. Shalako—Home of the Sacketts." Twelve miles farther on, along a twisting road that leads to Hay Gulch, is another sign, which is more to the point: "No Inspectors allowed on this Property. This is Our Property. We are capable of minding our own business. King Coal Mine. This way please."

Down a road covered with dust from the coal mine perched on a hill above it, a seventy-two-year-old great-grandmother, six feet tall and weighing 190 pounds, stood in the midst of her flower garden, snipping off the dead blossoms from her rosebushes.

"Me and old Smith have owned this mine for forty-two years," Violet Smith said, "and I've run off sixteen of those goddamn federal inspectors in the last six. One I chased with a gun and took after another with a two-by-four. I kicked their ass out of here. I don't need 'em anyway. I never had any trouble with the state; it's them feds that showed up in '71. I remember the first one—a bastard—he came out and said we needed a methane monitor. Well, we didn't need it; we've never had an accident in forty years. No equipment to put it up and no purchase order either. Well, the bastard said, I'm gonna shut this mine down right now, and he took off up the goddamn hill to see that the men didn't go back to work. I went up and said, Come on down to the office and let's talk it over.

It's too damn late, he said. It's not too damn late to choke you to death, you S.O.B., I told him, and yanked him out the door because I couldn't hit him enough in the car. Well, he wet his pants while he was still in the car and I got him down on the ground and gave him what for. I would have killed him, but he escaped and went to town and had papers served on me by a federal marshal, a big black guy. Well, I just punched him in the gut and told him I wasn't guilty of a damn thing."

Violet Smith smiled sweetly, gathered up her flowers and went into the house, which also serves as the office for her coal company.

With Irvin, her gentle, soft-spoken husband of fifty-five years, "Violent" Smith, as she calls herself, has worked in the coal mines, dragging her five children after her when they were babies and putting them to bed in the coal cars.

"Oh, hell, honey," she said, "I packed in the dynamite, loaded the coal, drove the old horse out and took him back in and shoveled away the garbage while old Smith was standin' around."

She worked underground for twenty-six years, then began to drive the big eleven-ton loaders up and down the mountain, a job she relinquished to her son when she was seventy years old. But it was always Violet who ran the mine and Irvin who raised the children.

"It just seemed more natural that way," she said, fixing a lunch of chicken chow mein in the kitchen. "Old Smith was always better with kids than I was and I could always handle the miners better than he could." Half a dozen miners work for her and some have been

115

Above. "Violent" Smith, seventy-two-year-old coal mine owner from Hesperus, has gained national attention for beating up mine inspectors.

Right. The Twin Pines Coal Company, Rockvale, employs six miners under the direction of Joseph Carpine, bottom right.

there as long as fifteen years.

Her trouble with the federal government started in 1969, when, after a series of mine disasters in the East, Congress passed stringent laws involving safety for miners working deep underground. The federal inspectors fanned out all over the country, checking out the mines and

levying stiff fines, which, according to Violet, looked like the national debt. She rails against some seven hundred "stupid" mining laws currently in existence, which fill a dozen books weighing sixty-five pounds; she has them all flung in a corner of her kitchen.

The Smiths maintained that the severe inspection regulations for the big mines failed to take into consideration small mines like the King, which do not go deep underground but dig into the hillside. Two other small mines in the Hesperus area were forced to shut down, but Violet Smith stood her ground, not only beating up mine inspectors but defying eight subpoenas for federal court hearings. Across the bottom of one she scribbled: "You can damn well drive the extra 20 miles from Durango and hold it here if you want me to attend."

Support for Violet Smith has been strong in the mountainous country around Durango, where people have been buying her coal for years, currently at thirty dollars a ton. Bumper stickers have appeared with the slogans: "Don't Tread on Me," "Violet's Militia" and "King Coal Mine Forever, Total Government Never."

But her disputes are not always with the federal inspectors. Once five men from Durango came out and argued with her over the ownership of her coal scales.

"I run 'em off with my .38—the prettiest little thing you ever saw," she said, donning a hard hat for her afternoon visit to the mine. "They hauled me into court over that—assault with a deadly weapon. The judge sat there and looked at them and looked at me and then he said, You five big men ganged up on this one

old lady? Yeah, they said. No wonder she run you off, the judge said. She should have shot you. So I went home with my bill of sale and never heard from them again."

Another time Irvin ran off two men who had come to unionize the miners.

"It was his turn," Violet said. "We have never had a union here and never will. The union guys is just as scared to come in here as the mine inspectors."

At the mine, the men greeted her affectionately and called her "Granny," asking her about a vein they were working on.

"They're my boys," Violet said, watching them disappear into the tunnel in their little cars. "There's a fellow in Durango that wants to buy this mine on one condition—that I stay on to whip the inspectors."

"I got eighteen grandkids and sixteen great-grandkids. They come out here and yell at me: Go, Granny, go." She picked up a piece of coal and clenched it in her fist.

"One thing you got to remember, honey," Violet Smith said. "You can't let the bastards wear you down."

The Creede town marshal sat in front of the city's 1929 Chevy fire truck, a red garter on his sleeve, handcuffs dangling from his belt, his gun in its holster and a pipe stuck between his teeth. Along the sidewalk, the tourists stopped, adjusted their cameras and took pictures of him.

"I was on the L.A. police force for twenty-five years," Donovan Cullings said. "Out there I was just one man in 7,000. Here I'm the only one—I'm marshal and chief of police. I'm somebody. They're under my thumb—all 625 of them."

Above. *August Menzel, Westcliffe. "I've been a judge for thirty-six years and an undertaker for thirty, so I guess you could say I get them coming and going."*
Top right. *The Creede Drugstore.*
Bottom right. *Mineral County Judge Robert Wordell has had no formal legal training but read law at night.*

Saturday night and tore up the local bar.

Creede, founded in 1890 when N. C. Creede staked the Holy Moses mine in the rich district that soon became known as King Solomon's Mines, was for a brief period one of the most prosperous silver camps in the state, employing two hundred carpenters just to build houses. Six-shooters were local life insurance policies; gambling houses and saloons ran day and night and along the streets moved a colorful collection of characters, among them gunfighter Bat Masterson, con artist Soapy Smith and Bob Ford, the killer of Jesse James, who was himself killed in his own Creede saloon. To Creede also came purple-prose writer Cy Warman, who immortalized Creede with a poem that ended with the lines: "It's day all day in the daytime, And there is no night in Creede."

It is this kind of fantasy, now more than eighty years in the past, that creates a mystique for Creede, Cripple Creek and other raunchy frontier towns, raised to pseudo respectability by nineteenth-century journalists and perpetuated by pulp novelists and Hollywood's celluloid kings. Tourists flock to them by the tens of thousands, seeking authenticity in ruins and tangibility in trinkets, usually made in Japan. Tough towns grown soft are heavy with memory and old age; famous mining towns, laced with tourist dollars, can overlook the fact that their existence is based on whimsy, their future assured only as long as the mystique holds out.

"We that don't carry grudges get along fine," said Robert Wordell, hurrying out of his Standard station, in his stained and worn bib overalls, and heading up the hill to the Mineral

But Creede, wedged between two steep rock walls with West Willow Creek running through it, is a peaceable little town. The last time anyone was locked up in its one-cell jail was when one of the miners from the Emperius, up on the side of the mountain, got drunk one

Winnie Lindsay, rancher, leases eighty acres near Montrose. "I've worked in offices to make ends meet."

County courthouse to hear a careless-driving case. Wordell, forty, has lived in Creede all his life and has been its elected judge since 1962, hearing only minor offenses because he has no training as a lawyer.

In his little courtroom in the bubble-gum-pink courthouse built in 1948, Wordell waited for the defendant to arrive, impatiently hammering his knee with a gavel.

"When I started out, I didn't know anything about the law," the judge said. "I got a set of lawbooks and every night, after I finished at the station, I sat down and studied them, sometimes until one and two in the morning. I felt I owed it to the people to at least know what a felony was.

"They say I'm lenient and I suppose I am. I hardly ever send anybody to jail and I don't impose very stiff fines. Most of these people are my friends and what they do is not so bad, compared to your city crime."

While he was sitting there, the janitor came in and swept the floor and the county clerk, Chloe Rogers, came in and wanted to know something about license plates. Creede is the only town in Mineral County, some eight hundred square miles in all, 94 percent of it in national forest. There is only one phone for all the county offices.

"I've had quite a bit of on-the-job training," Robert Wordell said. "I remember the first wedding I performed. I didn't have time to read over the service and so I started right in when they got there. I read it like it was: 'Do you, John Doe, take this woman, Jane Doe, to be your lawful wedded wife?' "

He got up as the defendant came in. "I've improved a lot since then," he said.

Creede, like Cripple Creek, looks to another mining boom; unlike Cripple Creek, its mines never did shut down completely, not even during the lean years from 1931 to 1968. During that time Ben Poxson, owner of the Emperius mine and Bob Wordell's father-in-law, kept at least a handful of miners busy digging out zinc, lead and silver from what used to be Nicholas

Ada Gates, farrier, Montrose. "At $16 a horse, you have to shoe a lot of horses to make $16,000 in one year."

Creede's Holy Moses mine. But now, instead of the old $1.50 a day, miners make as much as nine dollars an hour, with an additional incentive pay of twenty-one dollars for every foot they dig out. Most of the eighty-five miners employed by Minerals Engineering, Ben Poxson's old company, and the 135 men employed by the new Homestake mine live in shiny trailer houses parked side by side, row after row, a block from Creede's main street. Nearly all of them are under thirty, most are college educated, and some say that the mining job is temporary until they find something better.

The farrier's truck rattled down the main street of Montrose, a once sleepy little town along the Uncompahgre River where the Ute Indians used to roam. Along the rich bottom lands, irrigated orchards still produce as much as twenty thousand boxes of apples from twenty acres; now, however, this land is sought by real estate developers who find more profit in acreage than in apples. Montrose has grown so fast that it now literally surrounds the last remaining farms, which defiantly resist incorporation into the city.

The farrier turned off on a dirt road leading to one of them and said, "I'm probably the only woman horseshoer you'll ever meet. It blew their minds at first, not only because I'm a woman but worse than that, I was in show business in New York for eight years. I said to hell with that and came out here."

Ada Gates at thirty-two had been in Montrose five years, ever since she got out of horseshoeing school.

"It started when I came to Vail and ran out of money and decided to stay and waitress. I had a horse and every time I tried to get a shoer he was always too busy and I thought: I can learn

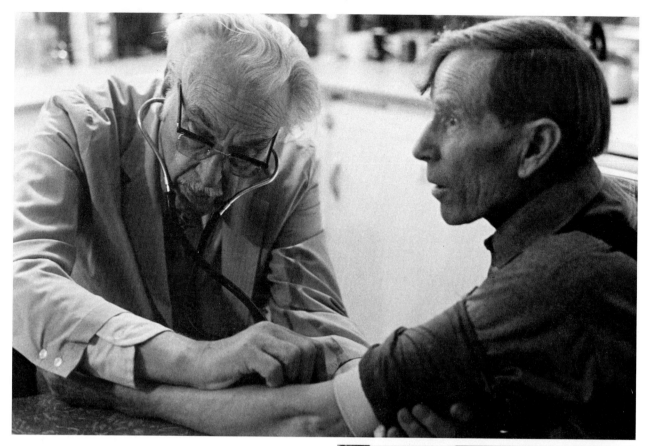

Dr. Norman Brethouwer is a second-generation Montrose doctor, who still makes house calls. "I kind of feel bad that I don't know everyone in town anymore."

Dr. Karen Dolby, Westcliffe, examines Helen Oldham in her office. She has been the only doctor in this remote mountain town since 1964.

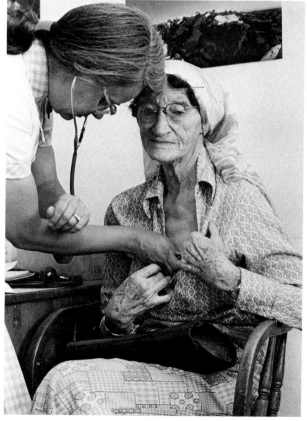

to do that. So I packed up my horse, Tupe, my six grand champion rabbits, and Dusty, my dog, and off we went to the Oklahoma Farriers School. There were forty-nine boys and me." Wearing no makeup, her once-long hair frizzed into an Afro, her designer clothes traded for a pair of Levi's and a cowboy shirt, Ada Gates was far removed from a career that had included doing stunt work in Westerns and working as Bob Dylan's road office manager.

If life in New York was tough, farrier's school was tougher.

"Bud Beaston was the teacher," she said, "and he came down hard on all of us to see if he could break us down. It's not a profession for weaklings or cowards. I cried every night for two months. I had horses stomp on me and sparks fly out of the forge and hit me in the eye and those forty-nine guys were rough, boy.''

Other training at the school included working at a forge, making corrective horseshoes and studying the anatomy of the horse's hoof and leg. There also was instruction on how to set a broken leg in an emergency and how to make a steel brace.

"I got through it all,'' Ada Gates said, driving through the gate of Roy Moore's eighty-acre ranch, surrounded on three sides by the city of Montrose. "I can make eight thousand dollars in six months horseshoeing, but it's a lot of work. Horseshoers only get sixteen dollars a horse. If I could shoe five horses a day, five days a week, I'd make forty thousand dollars a year. Men will run seven or eight horses a day and be comfortable. But I know my limitations. After all, women ballet dancers can't jump as high as men either.''

Roy Moore's land was being leased that year to Fritz Renfeld and his sister Winnie Lindsay, who had fifty head of cattle on it. When Ada Gates drove up, they were in the corrals, running their cows into a chute to be pregnancy-tested and vaccinated. When they were finished, Winnie Lindsay came out and held her twenty-three-year-old horse, Snoopy, by his reins while Ada shod him. Wearing a cowboy hat with a "McCarthy for President" button on it, Winnie said she'd been spending most of her time working for the American Agriculture strike.

"It's the first time in history that farmers have gone on strike,'' she said, pleased with the five hundred protesting farmers who had converged in Denver the week before. "We're feeding this nation and then some. If we don't get one hundred percent parity, there won't be a farm left in twenty years." She looked wistfully out across the housing development which had been farmland just a few years before. "Maybe there won't be any anyway,'' she mused.

Ada Gates banged out a horseshoe on the anvil with a hammer and said, "I bought seventy-three acres near Olathe and it's eating me up. I raised sugar beets for two years, but now I'm into growing malt barley for Coors. I've got fifteen acres cleared, but that's not enough. I've got fence to build and more irrigation to put in." She held up the shoe to see whether she had got the shape right to fit on Snoopy's hoof.

"I don't know, Winnie,'' she said. "Do you think women's lib means that you and I are going to get more money for what we do?''

Winnie Lindsay rubbed her horse's nose and looked around at Fritz, who was starting up his antiquated 1936 Farmhand Loader with its wooden slats in front for picking up bales of hay. "What I think is, we're going to do more than we ever did and not get paid at all.''

Every fall, when the aspen leaves turn gold and the high-country lakes begin to freeze over, the roads to the mountains are clogged with an army of camper trucks and vans, usually with a jeep in tow. This is the "hunting phenomenon,'' an annual pilgrimage to the mountains for the slaughter of thousands of deer and elk. Hunters, wearing electric-orange clothing and carrying hip flasks, two-way radios and plenty

Charles Stone and his mother, "Poker Alice," Ohio City. "I'm not going to any nursing home. No, sir, I'm not. Want to stay right here."

of cash, invade the mountains in the name of big-game hunting, a euphemism for whooping it up with the boys.

One bright fall day, a group of hunters from Oklahoma and California gathered in Chuck Stone's backyard in the old mining town of Ohio City and tried to load their balky mules. There were four of them plus a guide and they had packed enough supplies to last them a

An elk hunter loads up his mule at Ohio City.

month, let alone the three days they intended to be out.

"The reason we don't have women in a hunting camp is because the outhouse is just a board with two holes between two trees and the wind blows a lot," the guide said, tying onto the mule's sagging back one more sleeping bag and a pair of boots. He pulled the straps tight.

"What I say is, why bother with a board? Some guys is top-heavy. They don't know how to squat."

With that, the hunters rode off toward the mountains, lurching into a yellow cloud of aspen, kicking the mules in the side. When they were out of sight, Chuck Stone said, "You might as well meet Mom. She's ninety-two and mean."

"Poker Alice" Stone came out of the bedroom, scowling, her hair standing on end. She did not say a word until she had dished up her oatmeal, and then she said, "I'm not going to any nursing home. No, sir, I'm not. Want to stay right here. Play a little poker Saturday nights and do what I always done. Us women got to fight for our rights. I raised seven children, but three died. What's left want me to go to a nursing home. What am I going to do there? Who's in charge anyway? Gonna eat my oatmeal. Don't talk to me, Chuck. I'm not gonna listen to you. I voted for women's rights."

"Have a drink," Chuck Stone said, even though it was only ten o'clock in the morning.

"When I'm good and ready," Poker Alice Stone shouted, polishing off her cereal and holding her bowl like a shield. "It takes a long time to get old. People ought to give you credit for stickin' some things out."

But Chuck Stone, weary of combat, had gone outside and was trying to tear the door off what had been the Ohio City Jail.

"I'm for historical preservation," he said. "But that doesn't include my mother. Here, I want you to see the inside of this jail." But the door, nailed firmly in place, refused to yield. "How about some miners' shacks instead?"

In the little mountain towns with slopes too unmanageable to be appropriated by the ski industry or scenic attractions too subtle to be tourist meccas or a history too tame to be of interest to nostalgia seekers, there is a blunt honesty among the people that the mountains seem to have instilled. Perhaps it is because the winters are longer here than anywhere else, the highways are often closed and the people snowed in for days at a time, or perhaps it is the simple fact that high altitude has always pro-

Gay Williamson, ninety, Austin, has had the general store since 1920. "I was running the station till I got holes in both tanks. But I got free air, though."

duced a terse, no-nonsense response to life.

"When a fellow came in here asking for credit, I always looked at his pants. If the seat was worn, he didn't get it. If the knees were worn, he did."

"Go blow your nose between two rocks."

"He owned a dishpan, a brass bed and a gun, but he gave the gun away."

"Everyone knows that Shirley's a hard

woman. She never smiled in her life. Maybe she smiles on the inside, though.''

"I wouldn't say I'm patriotic, but every time I see the flag, I get a lump in my throat."

"Why should I have to get dressed up? It's good enough for who it's for."

Even the cemeteries reflect the staunchness of the mountains, which no man ever really matched, no matter how tough he thought he was. On a hillside near Rico, overlooking the lush tranquillity of the Dolores River, there is a headstone for a miner named Lazelle who was born on November 20, 1869, and died April 9, 1897. On one side of the monument the miner's wife inscribed a bitter message to the dead man: "STUART—This world would not have been so dark my dear, if you your thoughts had let me share. SADIE.''

Rico, at nine thousand feet elevation, is on the verge of death itself; the wind whips down a string of false-fronted frame buildings along a

Top left. Wooden sidewalk at Pitkin is the last in Colorado. Bottom left. Backyards in Rico are used for target practice. Above left. Back-road grocery store, Canon City. Above right. Along Route 50.

rutted street; torn lace curtains blow at the cracked window of what had been a miners' boardinghouse; the hotel is boarded up, the last saloon closed; even the gasoline station and the liquor store seem from a different time, a different intention. As late as the 1920s, horse thieves were active here and often were pursued by posses in automobiles and on motorcycles. But there is almost no one around anymore to give credence to the old days, to take the little facts that belong to Rico and bring them alive so that somebody cares, remembers and passes them on.

In his twelve-by-ten-foot cabin with a kitchen added on, Rob Snyder set down a pail of milk he had just taken from his cow, moving a crock of sourdough to one side. He fished a fly

Tony Ferando, Rico. "I've seen this town go up and down, but now it's laying sideways most of the time."

Top right. *Donald Atkeah and Betty Johnson run the Shell station in Rico.*

Bottom left. *First Baptist Church of Rico.*

Bottom right. *Ruth's Laundry, Rico.*

out of the milk, then added a handful of coffee grounds to a big pot that already had grounds in it from the day before. He sat on his sagging bed with the legs in kerosene cans to keep the bugs from crawling up and announced, "I am the oldest one alive who remembers what Rico

was like. My father, Chancy Snyder, came to Rico in 1879 with the first wagon train when he was fourteen years old. My uncle George Snyder was three weeks old and he rode in the saddle-bag. My grandfather Henry Edward Snyder started the first hotel here and my aunt Adelia was the first teacher. Hers was also the first marriage and she produced the first child." He said it like a recitation from a history book, with its important passages underlined in red.

"My father worked in the mines, then went into the cattle business. I was born at the mouth of Disappointment Crick where it goes through Summit Canyon. I was a trapper first—marten, lynx, beaver and muskrat. I even caught nineteen lions one time over there in Utah. Well, in 1922 I went off to British Columbia and taught school for a while, then I met up with a fellow who said we could make a lot of money trapping. I knew the country pretty well because I'd gone on a three-month, five-hundred-mile canoe trip that summer. I said sure. I put up all the money and we set off that September, expecting to be out by Christmas. We were on a lake that was ninety miles long and three miles wide with nothing but a ten-foot boat and a little four-horsepower engine.

"On the sixteenth of December the lake froze solid and the battery to the radio went dead and there was nothing to do but put all the furs on my back and get out. It took us eight days and eight nights to go 150 miles across that country. We'd make two fires and get between them, then make a lean-to that reflected the heat. When your face would burn, your back would freeze. You never did get much sleep. We finally

131

When days are fair, Rob Snyder takes his pick and shovel and goes up into the mountains to dig for gold.

came to an Indian camp eight miles from a trading post that had a team and sleigh."

Rob Snyder had a face that the younger generation would call "mellow"; it had in it not only the pride of his family's history and the richness of his experiences, but a serenity as well. When he had finished his coffee, he went outside again and picked up some tools for the next thing he wanted to do.

"When I got back from uranium country in

1950, all I had was a wheelbarrow, a fry pan and a tent. And I began to do what I always should have done—prospect for gold right down there along the river." He walked up the path with his pick and shovel and a bucket to hold the gravel.

"You see," he said, "the river used to be seven hundred feet up there. That's where the gold is. The rain washes it down and what you do is learn to tell by looking at the gravel what is solid iron. That's where the gold is—placer gold they call it." He stared at the mountain as if it could tell him something; the mountain, because it had been looked at for so long, had the appearance of being noticed, with a certain notch in one spot and a crooked tree in another. Rob Snyder went up the hillside along the narrow path, looking over his shoulder several times to see if anyone was following him.

"If people knew where my gold was, they'd come steal it," he said, sinking his pick into the red earth. "There's a channel up there that looks pretty good. Ought to work it sometime. Oh, I've found some good nuggets here and there, not enough to make me rich. There's just something about it. When you pan a pan of gold and see those bright slugs, it does something to you."

His bucket full, Rob Snyder trudged down the hill, swinging his pick over his shoulder. When he got to his little lake, he emptied the gravel into his gold pan, a little bit at a time. Carefully, in order not to let the gold spill out but to let the gravel go, Rob swished the water around.

"Gold is heavier than water and heavier than

Washing the gold he has dug, Rob Snyder turns up a nugget the size of a pinhead. "It's not worth much, but that's not why I do it."

rock," he said. "It always stays in the pan. See." And he picked up a nugget about the size of a pinhead and stuck it on the tip of his finger. From the pocket of his overalls he took a medicine bottle, added some gravel and water and put his nugget in.

"My grandmother, Martha Jane, panned for gold when she got here," he said, turning his face to the sun. "She found a few colors, but it wasn't until '94 that she got her big strike. She was coming up the river with a load of cattle and she saw this place and staked a claim to eighty acres. She took a lot of nuggets out; so did my father. He found twenty-one dollars' worth in the first three pans.

"Well, that's become my private little mine," he said. "I never take out of it more than what I need. I've got me a few cattle and a little sawmill up there on the hill. The other day I built me a bridge to get across the river, so I don't have to get my feet wet when I'm out checkin' on my cattle. I'm seventy-six years old. I don't like to get my feet wet anymore. I don't like to take life easy either."

When he had finished panning, half a dozen tiny nuggets were in the medicine bottle and Rob Snyder said it was enough for one day, fifteen dollars worth, more than he had ever made when he worked at the Argentine mine, down the road a way. Back at his cabin, he dug through his bureau drawer until he found his poems, read through them, then selected one that he said reflected the way he felt.

The seasons may come and the seasons may go
Bringing the sunshine, the showers, the flowers and
*   snow.*
My body may weather and weaken, but my
*   spirit shall never grow old*

Olive Truelson, Dolores. "I've got 350 head of cattle and one son. Don't know which was harder to raise."

Working in my Happy Little Kingdom
Working by the River of Gold.

A mile or so from Rob Snyder's place, a figure on horseback came down the steep hillside, through the forest of aspen and spruce, driving perhaps twenty or thirty head of cattle; they went bawling into a split-rail corral, a little dog helping to herd them in. When the cattle were all penned up, the rancher stuck out her hand

and said, "I'm Ollie Truelson. I've been ranching by myself for twenty years, ever since my husband died. I run 350 head up here in summer, then down to Dolores in winter. Sometimes my son Val comes up, but he's busy, so mostly there's just me. Every day I ride up on the mountain to see what's run off in the brush or got out through the fence or got struck by lightning. I ship in fall and calve in spring, same as everybody else. No, I don't think about it being hard work for a woman my age. Why should I? Work is work. A woman can do it as well as a man."

When her horse was unsaddled and put away, Ollie Truelson went in the back door of her narrow wooden house, which was once a hay barn, through a room that had a pile of harnesses and saddles in it, then through one that contained a bed covered with a tarp. In her kitchen, at the end of the house, was a new refrigerator she had got when electricity came in the year before, but that was the only concession to convenience. Her washbowl and a box of wood stood in one corner, with buckets and dishpans hanging on the wall. The door was off the old Hoosier stove, but she said it didn't matter. She had become used to cooking everything on top of the stove, where she could see what was happening to it.

Old wooden cupboards were hung on one wall of the kitchen, and on the doors, both inside and out, Ollie had written her diary in pencil, beginning with 1923, the year she and her husband bought the place. The entries were simple and listed not only the dates that she came up for the summer and went back down

Ollie Truelson's kitchen is out of another century; her diary is written in pencil on her cupboard doors.

for the winter, but recorded the important facts of her occupation: "June 13 snowed hard everything froze cattle survived . . . Sept 12 went to twenty lost the squash saved the carrots maybe . . . little moisture this year 1931 . . . awful dry this year 1933 no rain since last July . . . rained two days lost one calf and the lettuce . . . 1944 selling a lot of beef this year for soldiers probably . . . August 5 lost a cow to lightning."

By the beginning of the fifties she had run out of space on the outside doors and began to write on the inside. Now they, too, were nearly filled up, with space for just one more year.

"It goes to show"—Ollie Truelson laughed—"that a person ought not to live longer than he's got room on the door for."

That summer the Dolores River ran dry out near Dove Creek, where it arches and twists before meandering across the Paradox valley into Utah. Weeds started growing up in the riverbed and the town appealed to the Army Corps of Engineers to bring them water from Utah the way they did in '54 when the last drought hit. But there was no water in Utah either, and the little town of Dove Creek figured it had at most a two-week supply in its reservoir.

Twenty miles out from Dove Creek, on a lonely, wind-swept mesa called Squaw Point, a farmer named Robert Young knelt in the middle of his bean field and began to dig at the soil with a stick. There was no subsurface moisture at all. Around him, his pinto bean crop had withered; the plants were no more than four inches tall.

"They're sorry this year," Robert Young said, getting up. "They should be eight or nine inches tall and flowering. But it hasn't rained in two months now and I don't think it's going to." He kicked the soil, raising a cloud of dust.

In the house, his five daughters, aged nine to nineteen, were baking a cake; his wife, Ocie, was making frosting in a bowl. There was a resoluteness about them, a gaiety among the girls, watching the cake and stirring a pan of grits intended for the evening meal. Robert Young had only eighty acres to his name, eighty acres on which to make a living—$1,100 in a good year. To make ends meet he did upholstering, and he had worked in a machine shop until he got a piece of metal in his eye; the other eye had been blind since he was four years old.

Later, after everyone had had a piece of cake, Robert Young went into the living room and his wife got out his mandolin and he began to play, bluegrass music which he had taught himself. He could play folk songs and a little classical music, too, but it was bluegrass that he liked the best. Robert played the banjo and the violin after that, Ocie keeping time with one bare foot on the rug. The girls giggled and ran outside.

"My father bought this land in the forties for taxes," Robert Young said. "I think he gave three hundred dollars for it. It was mostly sticks and stumps and it ain't all cleared yet. I've got twenty acres left to go. We've got an old International tractor that's thirty years old and we've got the five girls to help us hoe. That's all we've got, and in good years we get by with that."

"There's ways you can make it," Ocie said. "We've got a few chickens and we had a cow, but she died. I've always had a garden too, but this year it all dried up. We never did have water here. We go eight miles and haul it in a barrel." At forty-three she was still pretty in her homemade dress, with a look to her that meant

Top left. *John Lambert, one-legged Dolores blacksmith. His business card reads: "Lot friends. No money. No car. Little business. The only handout I want is the government's hand out of my pocket."*

Bottom left and above. *Robert and Ocie Young and their five daughters live without running water in a tar-paper house at Squaw Point, twenty miles from town.*

she could survive without water if she had to.

"Hay is up to three dollars a bale," Robert said, "so everybody is selling their cows. I used to feed 'em bean hulls to keep the hay expense down. When the pasture comes back we'll get us another cow. Meanwhile the girls don't mind drinkin' that powdered stuff."

"He can do anything, Robert can," Ocie said, pointing to the bobcat he had caught and skinned and hung up on the wall. "He put together an old Model A just from the parts he found. We're not as bad off as an old uranium prospector we know that lives up by Mineral Creek. He lives in an old car body and cooks in a hub cap. He cut a hole in the floor for a fire and he eats with his fingers. Once we saw an old dead rabbit laying there with maggots on it and he said it was his dinner. One good strike, though, and he says he'll have enough money to last him all his life."

Robert Young went outside and looked out across the fields shelving off into the desert; the air was yellow with the dust that had blown back and forth all spring and summer. The drought and a fungus called fusarium root rot had made the pinto bean crop in that part of southwestern Colorado about ten percent of normal.

"This dry old country," he said in the manner of a man who had grown used to such things. "It promises you everything and gives you nothin', or it promises you nothin' and gives you everything."

A flicker of a smile crossed Ocie Young's face. She, too, accepted the reality of what a drought could do. "People say to us, How come you don't go on welfare? Everybody else is. Well, Robert can still see good enough to work. And me and the girls can always sew." She thrust out her chin against the thought of such total defeat.

"And I won't sell the land neither," Robert Young said, scraping the dust with a thick-soled leather shoe. "You got to hang on. Next year it may rain." He turned his head automatically to the waterless, sullen sky as if he expected to see a cloud. And then:

"A man has got to have a place to come home to."

It was as simple as that.

MESAS

The land is overwhelming in its vastness and desolation. From a ridge, it is possible to see a hundred miles or more, across a wind-blasted terrain where sagebrush has taken hold (because of the sheep, the cattlemen say), where two thirds of its scraggly acreage is administered by the Bureau of Land Management (in favor of the cattlemen, the sheepmen say), and where oil shale development and strip mining threaten to create overnight boom towns.

The early settlers laced this unyielding land with their frustration by naming the places Bedrock, Paradox, Devil's Grave, Skull Creek, Bitter Creek, Bugtown, Camp Misery, Cockle Burr Creek and the inevitable Poverty Gulch. Their homesteads, like the homesteads of the plains, still stand as lonely witness to drudgery and pain, escape and expectation. Rotting houses snag the rolling tumbleweeds, broken windmills claw the stark blue sky, and out in the sage fields, embedded in dust, are the plows of failure which never broke anything except their owners' backs. With rainfall less than ten inches a year, agriculture has always been a losing proposition.

"There's only one thing wrong with this country. It's laying on its side."

"We got three seasons out here. Winter, mud and August."

"If God was gonna give a name to hell, he would've called it Moffat County."

If the land is tough, the people are tougher, forged by what little it has to offer, hammered out through survival and perseverance into an identity that is faintly legend. The people in northwestern Colorado have read the Western novels, heard the tales of how Butch Cassidy used to hide out not far from where they live, and taken from a huge overlay of frontier history exactly what they needed to set the individuality of their isolated lives. A horse thief was hanged in a cow camp a few years back; cattle were rustled down the banks of the Yampa River and into Wyoming within memory of most fifty-year-olds. Ranchers still shoot coyotes and hang their carcasses on fence posts; still talk about lynching "niggers," hippies and Mormons; still war with sheepmen—but it is now through litigation rather than with a barrel of a gun. The universal villain is the government, appearing in the guise of game wardens, brand inspectors and agents of the BLM.

Joe Haslim stood in the hot morning sun in front of the cow camp he had been coming to for half a century or more, and looked out over the great winding gash that the Yampa River had made through the rosy sandstone hills outlined in the distance.

"I don't feel like turning up my fingernails for the BLM," the old rancher said. "If they cut my permit, I'll just kill the bastards."

With that, he fished in the woodpile for the bottle of bourbon he always kept there, hidden away from his brothers, who did not drink. He helped himself to a generous swallow, complaining about the Bureau of Land Management, which had recently raised his grazing fee after nearly forty years at the same rate. He took another drink, then put the bottle back.

Boyd Walker riding out of his canyon ranch near Brown's Park.

"Getting mixed up with the government is like wiping your ass with a hoop," Joe Haslim said. "There isn't any end to it."

Not far from Haslim's camp, a fiery old homesteader named Hy Mantle gained a certain notoriety for shooting at white-water rafters when they floated past his ranch on the Yampa River. Mantle also enjoyed a reputation as a horse thief and once boasted that his entire horse collection had been "donated" to him by friends. His disposition followed him to Mexico a few years ago, where, it is said, he threatened some natives from whom he was trying to buy

cattle. Mantle was killed with a machete and his body shipped home—minus the head. His friends buried him down by the river at a spot he had already picked out—but they had to set a stick of dynamite in the rock first.

The past hangs heavily in this rugged, unpopulated country, uneasy now because of the outsiders who are moving into the Piceance Basin, on the verge of an oil shale boom that is expected to create instant cities of two hundred thousand people—more than there have ever been on this rough and scoured land. Already, the BLM has revoked nearly all its grazing per-

mits in the basin and ranchers who have held on for generations are being forced out. With them goes not only the free enterprise system, to which they have been fiercely devoted, but something of themselves as well. It is the last of an era in northwestern Colorado—and the grass roots people know it.

As one cowboy lamented, "Your cowboy life is just about over around here. Hell, it used to be a cowboy was the only hero this country ever had. But now you got your astronauts and Elvis Presley. There's nobody interested in what we do. That kind of thing disappeared when they took *Bonanza* off the air."

The country and its history have produced a kind of man who, if not a hero to the rest of the world, is a hero to himself and his friends. Whenever cowboys get together, the talk is not of women, politics or the world economy, but of cattle prices, local rodeos and what the weather has wrought. They are no longer willing to die for the herd or to sleep out on the ground, but they are willing to work seven days a week to get a job done. The recognition that came so easily in the days of Zane Grey, Teddy Roosevelt and Tom Mix is now passed around among

*Reuben Oldland, top right, rancher, Piceance Basin. His
daughter, Chris, and son, Jerry, above left and right, wonder
how soon the oil shale industry will force them out of the area.*

*Bottom right. Mace Cox and his son, Danny, Rangely. "I've
got nuthin' but old wrecks around here. This kid's the only
thing that's not on its last legs or dead."*

themselves, for their ability to rope a calf with
their horse at a dead run or to drive three
hundred bellowing cattle into a corral without a
single mishap. The pickup truck has replaced
much of the work a cowboy used to do on a
horse, but there is hardly a cowboy who does

not brag about his favorite mount, "who can stop
on a dime and give you nine cents change."

"Cowboy trust" has not changed much
either—a handshake is still enough to seal a million-dollar deal; a phone call is all it takes to get
a neighbor to come over for a day's work,
always without pay. Tradition is what makes
them not only defend the monotonous, low-
paying life they lead but justify whatever hardship they have to bear. There is a "cowboy
ethic" along with the "cow culture" that pre-

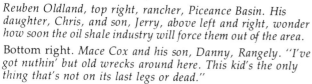

vails, and mostly it has to do with imitating how John Wayne behaves on screen.

The cowboys who are left are "more ragged than rugged"; more in love with the job than with the pay; and more likely to be buying land, a few acres at a time, not to satisfy their hunger for a place of their own, but to sell for a profit when the chance comes up. Most of them wear their sentiments on their bumper stickers: "Fight Smog, Ride a Horse," "Cowboys Do It on a Horse," "Eat More Lamb—10,000

Above left. *Albert Kirby, Rangely. "I don't know whether to vote for a Democrat who can't think or a Republican who won't."*

Above right. *Ruby Kirby displays some of her canned goods. "Last year I canned fifteen hundred quarts so the family wouldn't starve."*

Top left. *Justo Mofin, sheepherder. "Some say there is no difference in sheep, but I can tell them one from the other. I could not do the same with cows."*

Bottom left. *Hereford Haven Ranch, Hayden.*

Coyotes Can't be Wrong," and during the Johnson administration, "Eat Colorado Beef, Not LBJ Baloney." And most are given to pithy statements that are classics of originality.

Said Bob Hilkey at his place on Marvine Creek: "They used to call me the Marlboro Man. I didn't mind till I realized his spurs was upside down."

Said Gord Sullivan, down at his little ranch near Rangely: "My boss was so tight that if you ran a needle up his ass you'd throw both hips out of joint."

Said Ben Long, dressed in a zebra-skin vest in the Massadona bar: "You know what a dandy is? A fellow that's been circumcised with pinking shears."

On a lonely, wind-swept sage flat high above the White River where it meanders around a bend near Rangely, a covered wagon was parked conspicuously by a set of corrals and loading pens. The wagon, the kind that sheepherders use in the high country, was not covered with canvas, however, but with aluminum. There was no vehicle in sight, just two horses penned up in the corral. All at once the wagon door flew open and a lean, wiry man stepped out, took aim and fired his .30/30 across the open space. The blast reverberated through the air and Parl Jackson calmly put the gun down, picked up a can of Coors and tore the tab top off.

"Saw you coming," he said. "Reckoned I'd show you how good a shot I am. Hit that damn tin can the first time around. I don't believe no man ever walked that can shoot as good as me."

He threw back his shoulders, called to an old sheepdog named Bondi and went inside the wagon. There was a crock of sourdough on the bed, next to where he had dropped his rifle. The

Rolling a cigarette the old-time way, Parl Jackson says of his work, "I am one of the last professional coyote killers in the West."

wagon was tidy and on a little table was a bag of groceries, brought to him by his wife, who lived in Craig. "Yeah, I got a wife, sech as it is," Parl Jackson said. "She went off with my damn coat in her car." He began to roll a cigarette between his nicotine-stained fingers.

"I am one of the last professional coyote killers in the West," he announced. "Right now I'm workin' for this sheepman from Meeker. He

pays me ten dollars a head. Oh, I love coyotes. I wish there was ten thousand of 'em. I trap 'em, you know, by rubbing some of that coyote scent on poison meat. They love it, coyotes do, like it was some old French perfume. You want to try a little bit behind your ears?"

He put down his cigarette and the beer and started to trim his nails with a pocketknife.

"I been trapping coyotes going on forty years, ever since I was fourteen years old. Of course I rode a lot of buckin' horses and broke four or five thousand horses in my life too. If I couldn't ride a horse, I'd be a failure. I can ride any damn horse, any damn time."

He got up and looked out the window. "That old black horse is for my grandkid. I call him Kokomo. That red horse there is a race horse, worth twenty-five thousand dollars he is. He could beat anything in the Kentucky Derby next year—you want to bet? I could make a lot of money with him if I had the time, but I don't. Not with this here job killin' coyotes. Well, that

Parl Jackson, Rangely, in front of the sheepherder's wagon that is his home.

red horse there, I'll sell him to you for two hundred fifty. Want to see me ride?''

The race horse called Red stood with his back to the wind, covered with a canvas horse blanket, which Parl Jackson tossed on the ground. The back of the horse was scarred and the hair worn off from so much pressure in the same spot. The old coyote trapper threw a saddle on him and took off at a full gallop across the hard, dry earth. The wind was sharp and cold and the sun was nearly down; Parl Jackson was clad only in a shirt, but he did not seem to mind. He rode his horse back and forth, raking him with his spurs until a thin line of froth began to appear on the gelding's mouth. He stopped then, got off and poured some water out of a ten-gallon drum. The horse drank out of the trough, then Parl bent down and slurped the water that was left at the bottom. He stood up, wiped his mouth and said, ''I don't

like to see nothin' go to waste.''

He needed some more beer, he said, having gone through a six-pack in the last hour. On the way into Rangely to get some, he watched the familiar country going by, commenting on how he had once lived there and all the trouble he had gotten into because of it.

''I was trapping coyotes, see, on this ranch over there and they was tryin' to hold me for ninety dollars a month so I quit and went to work for a man for one-twenty-five. Then the war broke out. Hell, I wasn't gonna fight in no war, so I just saddled my horse and took off. They didn't see me for four years. I hid out all over—first in Cricket Wash up there to Craig, but it was too close, so I went deeper and deeper into that rocky country over there toward Utah. The FBI was after me all the time, but hell, all I did was turn the horseshoes backwards. They trailed me all over the country and couldn't get noplace. When I knew I was safe, I just hauled up on a rock and pulled them horseshoes off. Sometimes, just for fun, I'd catch me a wild horse and put shoes on him, then turn him loose and wait for the FBI to show up.

"Finally I heard that the war was over and I went to Salt Lake and turned myself in. They didn't believe it was me, figured I was dead. I think they wanted to let me go, but I'd broken the law. Well, I served about six months in a federal pen, then come back to Craig, huntin' a job. All they needed was a dog catcher and I said, Hell, I'll apply for that. They wanted to pay me a salary but I said, No, I'll do it by the dog—ten dollars each. How many dogs you got? Well, they said about two hundred, and right away I went to work. Within a week all them dogs was gone. They paid me, all right—I think it was two thousand dollars—but they wanted to know how I done it. That's my business, I said. They figured I was just a dumb old sheepherder. I never did tell 'em." He laughed and sat on the edge of the seat, wondering whether to divulge his secret. He smoked his cigarette all the way down to a stub before he said, "I just rubbed some of that coyote scent on my boot and led them dogs out of town and shot 'em in the gulch.

"Coyote scent, hell. It's made of their damn urine, you know. You can catch about anything with it. Except, of course, a woman."

When Blanche Miller came into Moffat County and bought the little grocery store and a half-dozen run-down cabins that hunters use during deer season, people wondered how long she would last on that barren stretch of U.S. 40 that runs from Craig, Colorado, to Vernal, Utah. A mile or so away, Frieda Patterson already had a gas station, the post office, a few rooms for tourists, a pool table, an antique shop and a lunch counter famous for a ten-cent cup of coffee and her delicious homemade pies. But Blanche Miller, operating out of what people call "lower Elk Springs," began to make hamburgers that weighed a half pound and served them on homemade rolls the size of a dinner plate. She also carried copies of *True Detective, Playboy* and *Oui,* and didn't mind the browsers who came in. Best of all, Blanche Miller acquired a reputation as a mechanic; on most days there was at least one rig parked outside her door, waiting for her to grind the valves, adjust the brakes or fix an oil leak.

"I've been here eight years now," she said one day, stroking a five-day-old piglet she called Dumdum. Her loud voice boomed across the small room. "Maybe I'm gonna stay and run for county commissioner. Straighten this damn place out. Look at this sweet little thing. The old sow tried to kill her. Hard to believe she'll be 450 pounds in a year." She bent her face to the little pig, who squealed and ran up her arm.

"I'm the best damn mechanic there is. I was an aircraft mechanic for twenty years, out in California. I was the only woman that held a senior rating. Hell, I can fix any damn machine in the world better than any man. Oh, I was married once, but I came to the conclusion that men just get in the way. Out here I have to do the work of a man. I even learn to think like a man when it's twenty below and the road's iced and

Ben Gillaspie, Dinosaur. "I'm going deaf. I can't hardly hear my fiddle anymore."

every damn trucker between here and Jensen is on the CB screaming for me to come and tangle him out. Ain't that right, Dumdum?"

The pig squealed and ran across the concrete floor and Blanche Miller got down on her hands and knees to coax it out from under the table. "She takes a bottle six times a day, just like a baby. Only difference between her and a kid is, someday I'm gonna eat her."

Behind Blanche Miller's store, a freshly slaughtered pig was hanging on a hook, getting "bled out" so she could cut it up when she had time. Nothing went to waste, not even the head, which now stared balefully up at the sky. In the kitchen, Blanche Miller had her recipe for head cheese already posted. It read:

"Boil the head and tongue of a pig in water 3–4 hours till done (depends on size of head). Cool. Take meat off bones. Dice all but tongue. Season with salt, pepper, garlic, onion, add

enough blood to make it stick together (pig's blood that you caught while you were killing it). Stuff stomach with seasoned meat (tie one end of stomach off), placing very carefully tongue in middle of stomach. Force rest of meat around it. That way when you go to slice it, you always get a piece of tongue. Tie off other end. Place in kettle of water to cover and boil 3 hours, testing doneness by taking toothpick and sticking stomach. If there's any blood, cook it longer. Serve with horse radish and mustard."

DINOSAUR, the road sign says, and as further proof there are streets named Stegosaurus, Brontosaurus and Pterodactyl. The town looks as old as its name, which used to be Artesia in the days before the Interior Department set up its headquarters for Dinosaur National Monument there. Only a few hundred people live in Dinosaur, a sun-baked little town not far from

Janet Kent, Dinosaur.

the Rangely oil fields, which have attracted what old-timers call the "wrong element," meaning brawny young men in fast cars and expensive pickups who get drunk on Saturday night and who have been known to shoot at livestock just for something to do. Dinosaur, without a motel, a restaurant or even a very good service station, is what so many towns along U.S. 40 are—a place between where people go.

On a side street in Dinosaur, which could have been a side street anywhere except that here it was dustier and the houses had the look of profound neglect, there was a green tar-paper shack lost amid a heap of junk piled from the door to the road. A curl of smoke came from the lopsided chimney, burglarproof metal screens were across all the windows and an assortment of washing machines, tires, easy chairs, apple cider jugs, cable drums and rubber boots was

arranged surrealistically on the front porch. Inside, an old man was making a fiddle with nothing but an ax, a pocketknife and a saw.

"What I want to do is make fiddles. Just make fiddles," Ben Gillaspie said, holding the rough-hewn fiddle in the air. "I can't hear good. Can't see good. Still, nothin' I'd rather do than make fiddles. Reckon I made four or five hundred fiddles in my day. This here's bird's-eye maple. They call it that because it don't have much heart in it, just a little old bird's eye in the middle. Sometimes I use an old piece of cow horn for a tail board. Sometimes I use wood." He put the half-made fiddle aside, then took one from the wall.

"My favorite's this one," he said. "I made it out of my mother's breadboard, some regular old wood from Kansas. It's the best fiddle I ever made on account of the sound and the way it plays." He picked up a bow and began to play a

The one-room Brown's Park school sits along a lonely stretch of road forty miles from the nearest town.

Mr. and Mrs. Howard Sadlier and their son, Cory Pence, a fourth-grader. "I've got a little copper mine I work back there in the hills. We don't have plumbing yet but someday I'm going to put a washing machine in."

tune. "I'll sing it for you if I can get the words in my face." He played "The Dying Cowboy," "The Old Oaken Bucket," "The Arkansas Traveler" and one he had made up, called "The Sheriff Sat on an Old Rusty Nail."

He sang them all in a row without stopping and when he at last put down his bow, he said, "I'm a fiddle-maker, not a violin-maker. Be sure and get that straight. A man that makes violins, he makes them with his head. A fiddle-maker does it with his heart."

He picked up his fiddle one more time. "The trouble is, I'm going deaf. I can't hardly hear my fiddle anymore."

Near Maybell, population fifty, more or less, there is a sign on the road leading west: "No Services Next 100 Miles." Forty miles along this road, in the midst of sagebrush flats, rising sandstone buttes and creek beds turned to sand, is the one-room Brown's Park school. But there is no town and never was; there is just this wild country that was home to Butch Cassidy and the Wild Bunch, professional killer Tom Horn and gun-toting cattle queen Ann Bassett. Before that, Indians traded along the Green and Yampa rivers which flow nearby and before that, the first fur traders sought a way through the labyrinth of canyons. Almost before everything, there were dinosaurs slogging through the hot, wet lowlands. Now there is nothing for

miles around except the wooden school standing beside the lonely road that winds through the mesas and canyons before it wanders off into the Utah desert.

There were eleven children in seven grades and they came from Colorado, Wyoming and Utah. Most of them were from ranches, but there was one whose father ran a little copper mine, another whose father was a game warden and another whose father worked for the Park Service. There was no school bus, and the parents had to drive as much as twenty-five miles one way, four times a day, or about five hundred miles per week. There were no athletics, no after-school activities, no place to stop for a Coke that was not at least an hour's drive away. After the eighth grade, the children went either to private school in Utah or else to Craig, nearly eighty miles distant, which meant that some member of their family had to move in and rent an apartment so that the child could finish high school.

"Education is a hard-earned thing out here," said their teacher, April Mann. "The parents spend all their time driving. The kids get up at five or five-thirty, do chores for an hour, get here by eight, then have another hour of chores after school. I wonder if a city kid could do all that."

April Mann was twenty-three years old at the time and Brown's Park was her first teaching job, accepted because her husband, Mike, was a cowboy at a nearby ranch. She was in the midst of teaching her fourth-grade reading class, which consisted of one student. Elsewhere in the room the other grades were listening with

April Mann, twenty-three, chose Brown's Park as her first teaching job. She lives on a nearby ranch, where her husband, Mike, is a cowboy.

After dinner, Boyd Walker takes a nap while his wife, Wanda, listens to the weather report on the old Philco radio.

earphones to math tapes, playing chess or doing their homework. The room was quiet except for the shuffling of papers and an occasional cough.

When the reading lesson was over, April Mann got ready for eighth-grade English (two students) and said, "The real education is living in a place like this."

Not far from the Brown's Park school, a dirt road plunges off into the sagebrush and winds through the open country another thirty miles or so until it comes to a great yawn of canyon made by Vermillion Creek cutting its way through the sandstone. The land has the look of isolation about it. There is no litter along the road, no signs of any kind, no utility poles, no fences, no evidence of habitation. If there are cattle here, they are invisible somewhere in a pasture that can be as big as fifty square miles,   on land that has not changed much in a century.

Six hundred feet below, at the bottom of Vermillion Canyon, Boyd and Wanda Walker have a ranch that is sixty miles from the nearest town, ten from the nearest phone; in winter, they are snowed in two and three months at a time, cut off as they are from county-maintained roads.

"You get used to it," Wanda Walker said in her spotless kitchen, making chicken and

dumplings for the noonday meal. "We have a six-month supply of food and if we run out of meat, Boyd can always shoot a deer right there in the yard."

Boyd Walker sat with his teeth out, sipping straight whiskey and listening to the weather report on an ancient Philco radio. "I grew up in this country," he said. "I raised one daughter and an Airedale. My dad was old Brigham Young's private coachman. The first chew of tobacco he ever took in his life he stole from Brigham Young." He took off his boots and leaned back in his chair. "This is what I'd call informal country. Like your post office was located wherever a person had the most kids and got the most mail."

Walker had never been out of the area, but he'd gone to Craig a couple of times and to Meeker once. He'd met a lot of interesting people just living where he was. "I remember old Wiley," he said. "The only money he ever made was selling water to the sheepherders and whiskey to the Mormons.

"And old Pat, he had a bunch of horses, then he got so poor he couldn't feed them or himself. He couldn't buy cartridges either, so he'd just rope a colt and cut its throat and eat the damn thing."

When dinner was finished, Walker put on his denim jacket, saying, "I was twenty years old before I knew anybody but Levi Strauss made men's clothing." The stories and the one-line jokes were his legacy, laughter his reward.

It was time to do some horse trading, so Boyd Walker saddled his old red gelding and rode up the canyon into the wind, dragging a

Every day after school, Tuffy Sheridan rides his milk cow in from pasture to barn. "My dad says I ought to put a saddle on her, but bareback's half the fun."

mare behind his saddle horse. Tim Mantle was already there at the chute along the road, unloading the horse that he wanted to trade. When it came time for business, Boyd Walker squatted in the dirt to draw Tim Mantle a picture of his brand. When they were finished, the two men hunkered on the ground and complained about the dryness and the declining price of cattle.

"A fellow can't hardly make a living at this anymore," said Walker, who had had his ranch just ten years.

"Why do we do it, then?" asked Mantle, who was from a ranching family legendary in that part of the West.

Walker looked at him in astonishment. "Why, Tim, what else would we do with ourselves?"

Sixty-five miles away in Craig, the town nearest to Boyd and Wanda Walker, the impact of rapid energy development was already being felt. The construction of a giant power plant—expected to have a peak capacity of 1,520 megawatts—had brought in 1,400 workers and their families, nearly tripling the population. Craig, once a law-abiding, churchgoing little cow town without even a police department, was transformed into a "big city" almost overnight. Now it had a housing shortage, a sixteen-man police force and a skyrocketing crime rate. A state-financed study showed that between 1973 and 1976, crimes against people and property in Craig rose 900 percent and 222 percent respectively. Alcoholism increased by a reported 623 percent and child behavior problems shot up by 1,000 percent.

What the statistics did not show—and what natives were reluctant to talk about—were the social changes that had come upon them

Monty Sheridan hooks up team and feed wagon on his ranch at Red Wash. "It takes twice as long to feed this way but hell, what else am I gonna do with my time?"

in such a sudden, incomprehensible way.

"I got to lock my doors now."

"I could go to town and see everybody I know in one hour. Now I see nobody and it takes all day."

"My [property] taxes went up this year just so them fast-buck artists could move in."

"I got one kid left in high school and I said to her, 'You get mixed up with these outsiders and I'll break your neck.' "

"We're between a rock and a hard spot."

What Craig faces next is an influx of coal miners, hired to gouge out three million tons of coal a year in what has always been ranch and farm land.

Monty Sheridan had been rounding up cattle all morning on the same ranch along the Little Snake River where he had been born forty-six

years before, the same land that his grandfather had homesteaded shortly after the century turned. It was broken, sand-wash country with fields of gray-green sage stretching out from the river bottom toward the dark shape of the mountains twenty miles away. The late-September sun was hot and dust lay in a thick layer all across the land that Monty had been working with his three sons—Stan, who was twenty, Tuffy, seventeen and Rowel, the youngest at fifteen. Monty had never been able to afford hired help and depended on his wife and boys to do the ranch work with him. The boys enjoyed the work, but with profits low, Monty wondered if any of them would want to take over the two small ranches he owned, one on the Little Snake River, the other forty miles away at Red Wash. After working for years on a road-construction crew, he had finally paid off his mortgage. Now

Pitching unbaled hay, Monty feeds 150 head of cattle the old-fashioned way as his new wife, Ruth, drives the team. "She used to be a stewardess and I said, feeding cattle ain't no different than feeding all them airline passengers."

cattle prices were plummeting, and he wondered if he'd have to mortgage his place again to make ends meet.

With the cattle finally all headed in the same direction toward the corrals, Monty rode up on his sweating palomino and said, "If a man was smart, he'd never get mixed up in a life like this. But hell, I don't know much else. Neither do them kids."

It was clear that out in that part of the West, for a little while at least, it was not important to know much else. Back at the ranch, even his new wife, Ruth, a former airline stewardess, was having to learn the hardships of the cattle business. The thought of it amused him.

"There are damned few women who want to live on a ranch," he said, twirling his rope. "They think it's nice for a month or so, but then it gets monotonous for them because they can't run downtown and see their friends.

"I had a wife who hated it. She said, 'There's nothing to do—just raising kids and gardens, mending those damn Levi's and cooking the same damn stew.'

"Yeah, I told her. That's what there is and that's all you need to know."

Here on this rocky, wrung-out land there are still remnants of what the old West used to be and mostly it has to do with the wild-horse herd that roams on Douglas Mountain, a dry and rocky lump rising out of the Yampa River drainage. The wild horses have lived there for a century or more on about 450 square miles, most of it unfenced, competing with cattle for scarce forage and water.

For some the wild horses were a source of income, to be caught and shipped east for plow horses, or when tractors came in, to be rounded up for pet food. For others they were a source of transportation, to be captured and broken to do ranch work, for they usually outlasted the conventional quarter horse in sheer durability.

For still others the wild horses were a link with the romantic past, and thus involved a cer-

tain obligation. Sometimes that meant the building up of the herd with one of their own stallions from time to time; or feeding them during the harsh winters, when temperatures drop to fifty below and snow covers the grass for six months at a time, causing the horses to eat one another's tails and manes in an effort to stay alive.

For years Martin Foster has always cut into his own supply of hay in the winter and gone up to the mountain and laid out the bales for the wild horses to eat.

"I like those broomtails," Foster said. "Not that they're pretty. They're ugly, with those big heads and short legs and manes in need of a trim. I just like to think of the freedom they have."

Contrary to popular belief, the wild horses did not descend from Spanish mustangs of the seventeenth century. They were simply strays who wandered off from farms and ranches a century ago, went into the vast reaches of the mountain and "became wild." Most ranchers point out that the wild horses are remarkable only in their ability to survive the worst range conditions nature can provide.

The wild horses helped Monty Sheridan out of one financial bind. He paid for each of his children by catching wild horses, at an average of twenty dollars a head.

"Every time my wife got pregnant, I'd figure how many horses I had to catch to pay the doctor and the hospital bill. When old Rowel was born they was down to ten dollars a head and I said, Hell, that's too much work. So we didn't have any more kids."

When the drought hit the West, the Bureau of Land Management decided to remove the wild-horse herd from Douglas Mountain. They pointed out that 83 percent of its range was in fair, poor or bad condition and that cattle were a revenue-producing unit, while wild horses were not. They went about running them into corrals after cutting off their water supply, exhausting some horses to the point of death. At the end of one summer's effort, the BLM had caught only about fifty horses this way, so they got the 350 that were left by rounding them up from helicopters in the rocky draws and gullies where they had sought refuge. Once captured, the wild horses were offered for adoption, a BLM plan that has been something of a farce. Of the seventy thousand wild horses that roam the West, only three thousand have been rounded up and adopted—at a cost of $800,000.

Along U.S. 40 between Elk Springs and Massadona, there is an 86,500-acre ranch which has on it 735 head of Hereford cattle, nine saddle horses, ten wild horses, fourteen head of buffalo, seven Texas longhorns, a flock of geese, eight goats and a pig named Maggie McGee.

The ranch house, a five-room log cabin, is three miles back from the road, set among a windbreak of cottonwoods. In the yard is a variety of pickups, tractors, trailers, plows, balers and other agricultural discards. On the porch are hung several horse tails, a bullwhip, a pair of chaps made out of an Angora goat that once lived there, a skunk hide and a one-quart bottle with a baby's nipple on it, used to feed one of the orphan calves. The living room is long and bare of rugs; on the wall are hung a Fannin sheep head, a stuffed wart hog, the head and feet of an ostrich, the tusks of a water buffalo, a six-foot-long rattlesnake skin, a wild pig from Texas, an arrowhead collection, a lariat made of wild-horse hair, and an oxen yoke. The adjoining utility room has a zebra head peering down over the freezer and a sable antelope head over the washing machine.

On the guest room walls are the stuffed heads of a huge, long-haired Highlander steer named Curly Bill, who used to be a pet, a hartebeest, a mule deer, and a dik-dik from Africa, flanked by a pair of moose horns six feet wide and ten pairs of various animal hoofs fastened to a board. A stuffed skunk lies on top of the pillows and a coyote skin is draped across the headboard. Under the bed, wrapped in a piece of canvas, is the hindquarter of a deer.

Minford Beard, a fifty-seven-year-old rancher, big-game hunter and something of a local celebrity ever since PBS made a movie about him and Monty Sheridan for public television, dragged out the hindquarter and carried it to the kitchen, where he whacked off some steaks with a cleaver and threw them in a pan of sizzling lard.

"We don't kill any coyotes or rattlesnakes on this ranch," he said with a sly grin. "The coyotes'll kill the sheep and maybe the rattlesnakes will kill a sheepherder, if he's a Mormon."

He slammed a lid on the meat and turned to his wife, Judy, twenty-five years younger, who was making cookies out of cow feed to eat with their noonday dinner. During the morning she had skinned a coyote to make into a hat, hol-

Martin and Louise Foster, Douglas Mountain.

lowed out the body of an armadillo to make into a dish, hung up a rattlesnake skin to dry and strung together a necklace made of shark's teeth. She was also making a suit for Minford to take to New Zealand, where, for the first time in their many world-wide hunting expeditions, she was going to pick up a gun and shoot an animal herself.

"Minford's always done the shooting," she said. "I was content to go along and take pic-

Above. *Minford Beard, rancher, Elk Springs. "When I die I want my hide tanned and made into a woman's riding saddle. That way I'll always be between the two things I love the most—a good horse and a beautiful woman."*

Opposite. *Judy Beard's duties as a ranch wife include feeding orphan calves and hauling hay.*

tures. But now I want to kill a tahr—to hang on the wall above my bed."

She had filled four big scrapbooks with pictures of where they'd been—to the Arctic Circle to hunt walrus, to Africa for lion and zebra, to Alaska for bear, to the Yukon for bighorn sheep, to Australia for water buffalo, to New Guinea

for rusa deer. Their hunting trips were geared to the times when there were lulls in the ranch work. Once it had been Minford's desire to get one of every kind of animal in the world and to build a trophy room to house them all, but now, with so many animals protected, he had given up the idea.

"I don't think hunting's so bad," he said, turning the deer steaks, which he called "buckskin." "Not if you do it right. The animal is going to die anyway."

Cowboys live every day with death and accept it with little fuss. When Minford's mother died the previous winter, he took a shovel and buried her himself in the family plot, about half a mile from the house, next to his two brothers, one of whom died from blood poisoning and the other from tick fever. He was making her a headstone out of marble he had lugged up from Marble, Colorado. He was in the habit of marking other graves too—the old Yampa River hermit Pat Lynch, a boy who drowned and a squatter named Waterhole Charley. He marked them with steel plates that he cut out with a welder.

At dinner, the talk turned, as it always did, to Minford's life as a cowboy.

But he was not just a cowboy—a man who works for wages. For twenty-five years he had had his own ranch, which he sold a few years back for $300,000, investing the money to pay for his hunting trips. Not long after he sold out, he was on his way to live in Canada when two friends of his from New Orleans asked him to manage a ranch they had just bought. It turned out to be the Three Springs Ranch, originally homesteaded by his grandfather in 1895. Min-

In their bedroom crowded with stuffed animal heads, Minford and Judy Beard figure where to put a new trophy. "We've just about run out of wall space. I either have to stop hunting or build me a trophy room."

ford agreed to take the job simply because he liked the work and the free and open life he has always had.

Minford Beard started in the cattle business in 1934 at the age of seventeen, when he plunked down a month's wages (thirty dollars) for a cow and leased four hundred acres of grazing land for fifty percent of his profits. He added to his modest investment whenever he could, selling wild horses and entering local rodeos. He enlisted in the navy in 1942 and when he returned in 1945, he took his entire savings of five thousand dollars and put it down on three thousand acres, two hundred head of cattle and twenty-five horses, which cost a total of thirty-six thousand dollars.

"In those days, that was all it took for a man to set himself up in the cattle business," he said.

"Today a similar operation would cost a half million to set up. There's no way a fellow is going to make money in the cattle business today. No way, not even if every cow has three calves."

Simple arithmetic shows why.

Three Springs Ranch, with its 17,500 deeded acres and 69,000 on BLM and Forest Service permit, is worth about $875,000 on the market today. With 100 acres needed per animal unit, Beard was running only 735 head that year. At that rate, the cost of enough land to graze just one animal unit would be $1,170. But there were other expenses (feed, which ran $32,000 the year before, taxes, interest, wages, upkeep, machinery, grazing fees), which raised the average cost of producing a single head of cattle to $250. At the previous fall's price of 33¢ a pound, this amounted to about $115 per animal, or a net loss of $135 each.

So much for the economics. So much for the facts of ranch life, which make the cowboy an endangered species. If Minford Beard and his friend Monty Sheridan are the last of a breed, as they like to think, then what they have done is already history, part of the legend that surrounds that part of the West and sets it apart from the rest of the country, where "progress" has ruined the land if not the imagination. A cowboy need only to be reminded of facts to realize that he is going the way of the dinosaur and the wild horse.

Minford took a toothpick to his teeth and said, "Your cowboy is pretty much a thing of the past. It used to be a cowboy was on horseback all the time, but no more. Nowadays he has to be a veterinary, a fence builder, a welder, an electrician, a road builder, a mechanic, a plumber, a hay baler, a carpenter, a post hole digger and a dozen other things that don't require a horse. In the old days, a cowboy considered himself above all that. If you handed him a shovel, he'd quit. Digging post holes was the lowest job on the ranch—that and fixing windmills."

Minford Beard got up to finish the day's work. He and his foreman, Jack Brewer, would separate the cattle they had rounded up that morning, weaning the calves from their mothers. Judy looked out the window and waited until his pickup was out of sight, then went to the freezer and found, stashed among the hides of a raccoon, a coyote and a skunk, a tin of Copenhagen snuff. She took out a pinch

and stuffed it between her cheek and gum in a little wad.

"My only vice," she said. "Minford would kill me if he knew." She went back to work on his suit, stopping after a few minutes to run to the sink and spit out the juice. Before the day was out she would have finished the front and made some buttons out of the horn of a caribou Minford had shot in the Yukon, helped to vaccinate 150 head of cattle, written in the diary she has kept for years, used a chain saw on a juniper tree, cut Minford's and Jack's hair and made a wind chime out of cow bells. Still, she has her list of chores from last year that never do get done: "give Gram choke cherry jelly, darn socks, make horn bracelets, skunks—skin and make hats, putty windows, winch truck, haul tree, make litter bug signs, make two pillows 12 x 10 x 4, make foot scraper for Minford's boots, sack up manure."

Judy Beard is given to endless lists. Fastened to the refrigerator was her monthly shopping list: "muskrat skin, glass eyes, $40 coyote—send money, goats, trigger, worm medicine, lanolin for cow's tit, 1¼ or 1½ steel bit, good fence pliers, steel trap."

"I don't need luxuries," she said. "I just need to know I've got a good man and some land we can prove up on. When I die I'd like to know I left a place better than how I found it. That's my definition of a successful life."

Minford Beard also has strong feelings about being connected to land that goes back a hundred years to his grandfather's time, about what he has done for a place by putting himself into it. There is something inestimable about so much time spent in verification of a life that is now nearly obsolete.

"When people my age and a little bit older and a little bit younger die off, there's nobody around who'll know the life we lived," Minford Beard once said. "There's no way. I don't know if we were any better having lived that type of life. We just have knowledge of our own time. That's all you people would have. You'll have knowledge of a different time."

To the grass roots people, knowledge of their own time is enough.

A GRASS ROOTS
GLOSSARY

apple, biscuit, noodle: saddle horn, pommel

belly up: to go broke

broomies, wrangs: wild horses

cobbled up: improvised, thrown together. "It was a cobbled up outfit we made of brush and baling wire."

come to your milk: to come to one's senses, wise up

dead from the ass both ways: too lazy to work

dough gods: biscuits

dude: a city person unfit for cow work. "That dude got his saddle on backwards."

gap and swallow food: any kind of soft food hated by cowboys (oatmeal, pudding, vegetables)

good hand: the highest form of praise one cowboy can give another

hair in the butter: a delicate situation. "When I found my Angus bull in with Shorty's Herefords, it was hair in the butter."

haul out: to leave, often in anger

henskins: thin boots or blankets

mill tails of hell: to suffer a hangover

Montgomery Ward: a dude's way to catch a horse or cow by tripping it with a rope strung across its path

Mormon rig: a poorly done job; an improperly saddled horse; anything inferior. "That fence looks like a Mormon rig."

nobody tops my horse or rides my circle: "I carry my share of the load."

old sister: worthless old cow; can also mean an undesirable woman

old yos, breggs, woolies, Mormon crickets: sheep—the lowest form of animal life, as far as a cowboy is concerned.

outfit: anything owned by a cowboy including his clothing; e.g., horse, ranch, truck, saddle, rope, tractor, branding chute, rifle.

quinine: a creature or a cowboy who doesn't measure up

really boatin' down Big Sandy Creek: heading back to camp in a hurry

rimfire: to do a dirty trick to one who has it coming. "We rimfired Danny's horse" (loosened the saddle so Danny would fall off).

rode hard and put away wet: exhausted, not properly cared for; horse terminology applied to people. "You look rode hard and put away wet."

she stuff: anything female, animal or human. "I bought some she stuff [cows] at the auction Saturday." "When I came to this country, it was short on she stuff [women]."

sow coon: bad storm

spraddled out: to rest, catch one's breath, on the ground

stayed out with the dry cattle: had a night on the town

stove up: stiff and sore

swole: stirred up, had enough. Applies to people and cattle. "She's swole."

throwed in with: became partners, in business or marriage

tooley-wads: boondocks, back country

twine, string: lariat, rope. "Pull down your twine" (Get ready to rope).

ACKNOWLEDGMENTS

For almost two years, as I traveled thousands of miles on lonely Western roads, a number of people taught me what they knew about the land and its history, shared remembrances of their lives and invited me into their homes for meals. They appear in this book, not as subjects but as friends to whom I give particular thanks. Others, hearing about the project, volunteered to introduce me to relatives and friends who they thought deserved to be in the book. Among these rural assistants were Calvin and Janetta Evins of St. Francis, Kansas, who knew many families on the plains of eastern Colorado; Margaret Lucero of Antonito, who not only introduced me to the gracious Spanish people of the San Luis valley but translated their language for me; young Andy Pleasant of Dolores, who accompanied me to Rico; Judy Beard of Elk Springs, who knew everyone appearing in the "Mesas" section; Mary Ann Gossett of Watrous, New Mexico, who found all the great people who make up the Mora River section of this book; and Denise Garcia of Watrous, who shared her relatives with me and provided the much-needed translation. Ruth Wild's knack with people in Cripple Creek and Victor—and her knowledge of its history—made it easier for me to finish that last section of the book in the winter of 1978.

But *The Grass Roots People* project would not have come into being at all had it not been for Naomi Stewart of the Colorado Centennial-Bicentennial Commission staff. I am grateful to her and to Robert Sheets, director of the Colorado Council on the Arts and Humanities, for funding that has made this book possible.

A further grant, from the Colorado State Historical Society Foundation, allowed me to continue work after the CCBC funds ran out. I thank Janet Lecompte of Colorado Springs, who was responsible for this generosity.

Bea Vradenburg, the dynamic manager of the Colorado Springs Symphony, was an early supporter of this project in its conceptual stage. I also wish to thank Alan Hazlett of Shewmaker's Camera Shop; and Andrew Taylor of Colorado Springs, who processed the film and made all the prints, including the exhibition at the Heritage Center in Denver. His commitment to this project has been nearly as large as my own.

Somewhere along the line, I married one of my more intriguing subjects, rancher John Brittingham of Ramah. He not only provided much of the working ranch scenes but became involved in proofreading and picture editing. To him I give love and special thanks, and the promise that I will help him feed, round up his cattle and brand—but deliver me from witnessing one more horse-castration scene.

Thanks are also due to my editor, Ann Harris, whose enthusiasm and support have once again seen me through some dark moments; Edna Walker, my long-time housekeeper, who kept children and house together during long periods when I was on the road; and Helen Lynch, my indispensable, patient typist.